LORD OF THE DANCE

Lord of the Dance

The Autobiography of a Tibetan Lama

CHAGDUD TULKU

PADMA PUBLISHING

Published by Padma Publishing
P.O. Box 279
Junction City, CA 96048

© Padma Publishing 1992

First published in 1992

Printed in the United States of America
98 97 96 95 94   6 5 4 3 2

Cover design by Joanie Yokom
Frontispiece © Don Farber, 1989

Chagdud Tulku, 1930–
Lord of the dance : the autobiography of a Tibetan lama
ISBN 1-881847-00-4
1. Chagdud Tulku, Rinpoche, 1930- . 2. Lamas—China—Tibet—
Biography. 3. Lamas—United States—Biography. I. Title.
BQ946.A345A3   1992
294.3'923'092—dc20   92-23341
[B]   CIP

ISBN 1-881847-00-4 Paperback

I have no wings, but still I fly in the sky;
I have no magical power, yet like magic
I journey throughout realms of illusory display,
here and there, in nine directions,
exploring the connections of my karma.

Written in Mürren, Switzerland, by
Gargyi Wangkhyug (Chagdud Tulku),
whose given name means
"Powerful Lord of the Dance"

Contents

Contents

Contents

Contents

Foreword

CHAGDUD TULKU RINPOCHE came to America in 1979 and has resided here ever since. But from the time of his birth in Eastern Tibet, in 1930, to his arrival in the States, a story has unfolded as remarkable as any I have ever heard. This book is that story.

First, I want to set Rinpoche's story in some sort of context, for there are many things he simply will not tell you, even though this is his autobiography. He will not speak of his seemingly boundless compassion, a compassion that to us, his students, defines his very being. He will not talk of his profound awareness of the absolute nature of mind, an awareness he seems to be living and transmitting twenty-four hours a day. He will not tell you of the thousands and thousands of people whom he has served as teacher, spiritual master, physician and friend. He will give little hint that he is renowned as a scholar, artist and poet. Few of his remarkable accomplishments over the past decades—especially those in the West—will you find in this autobiography, and you cannot know from his narrative that this man has enhanced the lives of an incredible number of people through his profound transmission of the spiritual path.

When Rinpoche arrived in Los Angeles on October 24, 1979, he and his wife-to-be, Jane, first went to San Francisco. In mid-1980 he was asked to visit Eugene, Oregon, in order to teach an overview of Tibetan medicine to a group of American doctors. At the request of His Holiness Dudjom Rinpoche he remained in the Eugene area as a resident lama of Yeshe Nyingpo, the name given to Dudjom centers in the United States. Several years later, responding to students who wanted to ensure that there would be a seat in the West for future Chagdud incarnations, Rinpoche established the Chagdud Gonpa Foundation.

The original Chagdud Gonpa, founded in 1131, is one of the few monasteries in Eastern Tibet to have survived the Communist Chinese invasion. Chagdud Tulku Rinpoche, as the sixteenth incarnation of the original founder of that monastery, set up the first seat of Chagdud Gonpa in the West at River House (later renamed Dechhen Ling) in Cottage Grove, Oregon. There, as in all Chagdud Gonpa centers, instruction was offered in the methods and wisdom of Tibetan Buddhism, including the arts, philosophy and meditation practices of the Vajrayana Buddhist tradition.

In the fall of 1988 Rinpoche and his students acquired 286 acres in northern California's Trinity Mountains, and Rigdzin Ling, Chagdud Gonpa's main center, was born. The heart of the development at Rigdzin Ling will be a traditional Tibetan Buddhist temple, or *lha khang* (literally, abode of deities), which will include an extensive display of Vajrayana sculpture and decorative arts.

Presently, the Chagdud Gonpa Foundation has seven centers on the West Coast as well as centers in Brazil and Switzerland. Rinpoche's other projects include the Maha-karuna Foundation, which provides support for poor and infirm Tibetans in the refugee communities of India and Nepal; the Tibetan Library, which purchases and preserves rare and irreplaceable Tibetan texts; and Padma Publishing, dedicated to making the works of the Nyingma tradition available in English, as well as translating and editing Rin-poche's own teachings. He has also created major Buddhist statues in the United States and has trained several Westerners in Tibetan art.

Rinpoche travels constantly, stopping only to lead retreats. To those who urge him to slow down, he explains, "I am still gathering my students. Perhaps some of the dharma seeds I plant now will ripen in future lifetimes. Vajrayana bonds are very strong and are not dissolved by the illusory displays of death and birth. We meet and meet again until ultimately we recognize that we are inseparable in enlightened buddha nature."

When Rinpoche's family, students and friends began asking him to write down the experiences that make up this volume, he saw no reason to record his life. He said that he did not want to write the usual Tibetan *namtar*, an account of a lama's life in which human failings are glossed over by the sheen of spiritual attainment. Although Rinpoche is a *tulku*, a recognized incarnation of a highly realized lama, he himself teaches that *tulkus*, being born into the realm of humans, must deal with very human issues in establishing the con-tinuity of their spiritual path from one life to another. The essential attributes of a *tulku* combine a powerfully directed intention to work for the welfare of all living beings with the meditative realization to sustain this intention throughout this life and through the turmoil of the intermediate state between death and rebirth.

The combination of pure intention and great realization that produces a *tulku* also produces an extraordinary life, as Rinpoche demonstrates, and the requests that he write his story persisted until he finally yielded to them and began this book. He did not emphasize the achievements that have so defined his experience, but mostly his human foibles and his mistakes, using these to make teaching points, essentially at his own expense.

Anybody who knows Rinpoche will realize that he would write his story in no other way. Never mind that he is one of the greatest living masters of Dzogchhen, the Great Perfection, the highest Buddhist teachings. Never mind that he took the ground-breaking step of fully ordaining a Western woman as a lama or that he is one of the first Tibetan masters to take Westerners completely into his confidence and trust, and to train them according to the teachings of the Great Perfection. Never mind that all of his students have unlimited access to him literally twenty-four hours a day. None of this has made its way into the following pages. Although Rinpoche teaches many categories of Vajrayana Buddhism, his realization of the Great Perfection informs his presentation of every level of teaching and is at the heart of his transmission.

Of the three major categories of the Buddha's teachings, the first, Hinayana, emphasizes the basic meditation practices of concentration and insight, and sets as its goal liberation from suffering through renunciation and cutting all attachment. The second, Mahayana, emphasizes the path of compassion and selfless motivation to work for the benefit of sentient beings until all are enlightened. The third, Vajrayana, emphasizes the revelation of mind's true nature, using many skillful methods of which the Great Perfection is the highest and most direct.

Rinpoche's life demonstrates how Great Perfection realization becomes thoroughly integrated with the conduct of daily activities. Mind's boundless, absolute nature, nakedly apparent to him in moments of visionary experience as a young child, became the central thrust of his spiritual path thereafter in finding teachings that would allow him to stabilize those glimpses. Throughout his last turbulent period in Tibet following the violent conquest by the Chinese communists and during the difficulties of being a refugee in India and Nepal, there was a profound continuity in his spiritual perspective and a deep, powerful current of compassion. In one of his published teachings he says:

The key to all is pure-heartedness, one's own selfless aspirations, one's pure motivation. Your actions and those of another may not be so different; the difference is in the heart, in the motivation for what you do. And that's what makes all the difference in the outcome of your actions in the world. You must have the purity of your own heart, the purity of your own stance and intentions toward others and the world around you. This is the seed of all inner peace.

When one is in the presence of Chagdud Rinpoche, one is aware that this is a large-scale human being, a man of great qualities, humor and sincerity. As one of his students put it:

Sometimes he flashes forth with words that have a stunning impact, like a lightning bolt. Then, after the shock comes a freshness, like the clean air that follows a thunderstorm. The whole environment of one's being feels purified. As for Rinpoche, he is immovable.

His love is still there. His kindness is still there. The incomprehensible vastness of his mind that holds all the phenomena of our own is still there.

Asked why he finally wrote his autobiography after ignoring requests to do so for many years, he replied, "My life is a lesson in impermanence, and impermanence is the foremost teacher of the spiritual practitioner." Chagdud Tulku's story can be read on many levels—as a colorful, often humorous adventure story; as an inner, spiritual journey; and as a teaching on how one person attains the perspective of absolute truth amid life's uncertainty. As such it is both inspiring and encouraging, and highly relevant to anyone who seeks ultimate meaning in this time of dire prediction.

Ken Wilber
Boulder, Colorado

Preface

TIBETAN CONVERSATIONS and even dharma discourses are filled with stories, stories to pass time, stories to illustrate points. The stories of Tibet that I told to my Western students fascinated them and they often urged me to write them down. After entreaties from many people, the writing of this book was catalyzed by Lisa Leghorn. I told my stories on tape, and Tsering Everest, my interpreter, rephrased my English, which is still not perfect. My wife Jane Tromge then reworked the transcriptions of the tapes so that the oral narrative became this book. She received encouragement and editorial assistance from Lisa, Mary Racine, Bob Tajima, Linda Baer and many other people in a process I thought would take a few months but in the end has taken almost four years.

Now I am preparing for another journey into Tibet, again uncertain about Chinese permissions and the conditions we will find. At home—for the United States is really my home and I am a citizen—I have numerous students, many well grounded in spiritual practice. Artworks are being created, texts are being published and an enormous prayer wheel in California spins the blessings of hundreds of millions of mantras in all directions. Though the play of impermanence will gather and disperse, may any virtue endure and benefit forever.

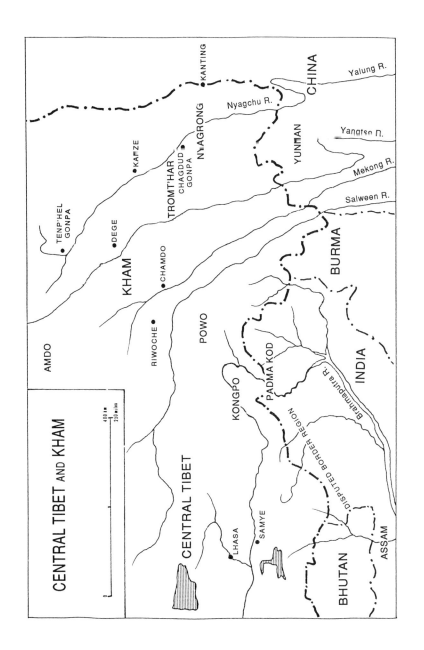

CENTRAL TIBET AND KHAM

CHINA

Yalung R.

KANTING

Nyagchu R.

YUNNAN

Yangtse R.

KARZE

TROMT'HAR

NYAGRONG

CHAGDUD
GONPA

Mekong R.

Salween R.

TENP'HEL
GONPA

DEGE

KHAM

CHAMDO

BURMA

AMDO

RIWOCHE

POWO

PADMA KOD

INDIA

KONGPO

Brahmaputra R.

DISPUTED BORDER REGION

CENTRAL TIBET

LHASA

SAMYE

BHUTAN

ASSAM

400 km
250 miles

0

xix

Prologue

THE LAMA had traveled several days by horseback from his monastery, along the narrow Nyagrong Valley with its deep forests and turbulent river. He had crossed the jagged mountains and the long, treacherous boulder-strewn ridge to this alpine valley and had honored the request of its leading family to do a wealth ceremony. Now he would return to his monastery, and these people would make their dangerous and costly pilgrimage to Lhasa, hopefully better able to afford it by virtue of this ceremony.

He took another sip of fiery *arak* and looked around the vast, black felt tent. Several hundred persons were eating, drinking and talking merrily in the total relaxation that follows the intensity of a great ceremony. And again he looked at the young woman.

She was very beautiful, not more than seventeen, and seated on a throne among the high lamas. In his meditation she had appeared to him as the deity White Tara, with eyes on the soles of her feet and her palms and one in the center of her forehead. Even now, through less visionary eyes, she did not appear ordinary.

1

He summoned her, and as curious faces turned their way, he handed her an exquisitely wrought reliquary box, a *gau*. "You and I have had only a brief connection in this lifetime," he said. "But in the future our connection will be very deep. Please accept this *gau* as a sign."

As the young woman took the *gau,* the lama's attendant monk took note. Some sixty years later he would say to the assembled lamas and monks of Chagdud Gonpa, "I never doubted that this Chagdud Tulku is who he is, because I was with him in his last life when he gave Delog Dawa Drolma, the one who became his mother, that gold and silver *gau.*"

1

Delog Dawa Drolma

M Y MOTHER Dawa Drolma was remarkable for her beauty, her fierce temper and her unconditional generosity. When she was a child, the family found this last quality most disturbing. "Venerable people, I am old, penniless and very hungry. Please, do you have something for a poor unfortunate one like me?" A plaintive plea by one of the numerous beggars who wandered up to the family tent would set off a flurry of activity. Someone would rush to the beggar with some *tsampa,* a bit of butter and perhaps yogurt; someone else would dash to Dawa Drolma to divert her from attending to the beggar herself. Others would station themselves protectively by the precious shrine objects and the various repositories of the family's wealth.

If relatives and servants couldn't restrain Dawa Drolma in time, or worse, if the beggars called when they were away, inevitably she would seize some valuable item from the family coffers—the silver offering bowls, a piece of Chinese silk, an auntie's favorite turquoise hair ornament—as her offering to the incredulous mendicants. Her compassion was limitless and she wept over their predicament. Her attachment to the family's wealth was slight, so they took to hiding it, even though they commented among themselves that the child's spontaneous generosity was definitely a sign that she was extraordinary, surely an emanation of the deity Tara herself, an embodiment of enlightened wisdom and compassion.

Our family, the Tromges, was a large clan that lived in the Tromt'har region of Eastern Tibet. Tromt'har is a high plateau, probably more than thirteen thousand feet in elevation. Pilgrims making their way from Tromt'har to Lhasa, which is at eleven thousand feet, used to complain about the heaviness of the lowland atmosphere. It is a region of glittering lakes, green meadows, alpine flowers and resplendent skies, and there the family's thousands of sheep and yaks were pastured. Our family, like most in that region, lived in black yak hair tents. Ours was a prosperous clan, and one of our tents was large enough to hold four hundred people. There was only one other tent that large in all of Eastern Tibet. Occasionally, when lamas and monks were assembled to conduct great ceremonies, the tent would be filled to capacity. The assembly sat in long rows on Tibetan rugs and sheepskins, with the high lamas on thrones at the far end, and everyone drank salt tea and made jokes until the ceremony began. Then, as the warm glow of butterlamps and the smoke of cedar incense filled the atmosphere, the deep chanting of the liturgy would commence with its awesome accompaniment of cymbals, drums, oboes, conches and horns, resonating far beyond the tent until it dissolved in the stillness of the thin air.

There were several highly realized lamas in each generation of the Tromge family, and my mother was the most famous in hers. She was one of Tibet's five great wisdom *dakinis*— female emanations who spontaneously benefit beings by their

4

activities. Terton Jigmed Khakyod Wangpo had prophesied her birth as an emanation of the longevity deity White Tara and an incarnation of Yeshe Tsogyal, Tibet's most revered female practitioner and the spiritual companion of Padmasambhava, the Vajrayana master who propagated Buddhist teachings in Tibet in the eighth century.

Dawa Drolma was also a *delog,* one who has crossed the threshold of death, traveled in realms of existence beyond those visible to us as humans and returned to tell about it. One day, when she was about sixteen, Tara appeared to her, not in a luminous vision but in person, and told her that she would soon fall ill and die. However, if she followed certain instructions explicitly, she would be able to revivify her dead body and benefit others by teaching about her experience. Soon after, Dawa Drolma had a series of bad dreams that revolved around three demonic sisters who were robbing all beings of their vitality. With black lariats and silk banners they tried to ensnare Dawa Drolma around the waist, but the deity White Tara prevented them from doing so by surrounding her with a protection circle. Eventually, however, the menace in the dreams was so strong that Dawa Drolma knew it foretold her imminent death. She went to her uncle, the great Tromge Trungpa Rinpoche, and with his help made the necessary arrangements, just as Tara had instructed. Then she became extremely sick and died, despite the efforts of the many doctors who were summoned.

Exactly as she had stipulated, in the presence of an attendant named Drolma her corpse was washed in consecrated saffron water and dressed in new clothes. It was carefully laid out in a room without a morsel of food or a drop of water. The door was draped in blue cloth, padlocked and sealed with the sign of the wrathful fire scorpion, and a man dressed in blue stood guard outside. Everyone was warned to refrain from any ordinary chatter, to recite only prayers and mantra. For the next five days and nights Tromge Trungpa, along with several other lamas and monks, did prayers and ceremonies continuously in the adjacent room. At the completion of this vigil, Tromge Trungpa entered the room where the corpse lay, cold and pale as he had left it, and recited powerful long-life prayers to summon Dawa Drolma's mindstream back into her body. In the account she dictated several days after her return, she described her reentry into her body:

When the consciousness reentered my physical body, I sneezed violently and experienced total disorientation. An instant later, I was in a state of faith and joy at the visions of the pure realm, and horror at the karmic visions of the hells. I felt as though I were waking up from sleep. Uncle Trungpa was standing in front of me, holding a longevity arrow and looking at me with concern in his bloodshot eyes. I was unable to say a word, as though I were a bit shy. Everyone was crying and excited, and saying things such as, "Wasn't it difficult?" "You must be hungry!" "You must be thirsty!" They were almost pouring food and drink over my head. Although I protested, "I feel absolutely no discomfort due to hunger or thirst," they didn't believe me. Everyone was saying, "Eat! Drink!" They all felt joy as immeasurable as a she-camel who has found her lost calf. We all partook of a feast to celebrate.

During her five-day journey as a *delog,* my mother's consciousness, unhindered by the constraints of a physical body, traveled freely through all the realms of mind, from the hell realms with their ceaseless, unbearable suffering, to the most exalted purelands of the wisdom beings. For the rest of her life, whenever my mother taught, she drew from her experiences as a *delog.* Her descriptions of the misery of the

6

other realms were very vivid, and tears came to her eyes as she spoke. "No matter how difficult your life is in this human realm," she would say, "there is no comparison between the difficulties here and those in other realms." No one doubted that she spoke from direct experience, and her credibility was enhanced by the messages she brought to people from their deceased relatives.

In particular there was a very wealthy businessman named Drilo whose sister had died and was now in a state of torturous suffering. By chance she encountered my mother and begged her to relay a message to Drilo, telling him the whereabouts of certain valuables she had secreted. "Tell my brother to use those things for ceremonies and dedicate the prayers to me so that I may find release from this terrible suffering more quickly." When my mother returned to the human realm, she sent a message to Drilo, but he was busy shearing sheep and refused—rather rudely—to meet with her. So she sent him a letter telling him where the valuables were hidden. Drilo was astounded, for only he had known that these things were missing. Upon finding them by the letter's instructions, he decided it would be worthwhile to meet my mother. Their meeting produced a second startling revelation when she informed him, "Unless you take certain steps, you will join your sister in the realms of hell."

Drilo replied, "If you can tell me exactly what to do, I will do it, but only if it prevents me from going to hell altogether. I won't do anything just to go to hell for less time, and I won't meditate. I'm a businessman, not a practitioner, and I won't devote my time to practice."

"Then I will be very direct," she said. "Each day you must sponsor at least a hundred butterlamps, each year you must sponsor a reading of all one hundred and eight volumes of

7

the Buddhist canon and in your lifetime you must sponsor the building of a *mani* wall." A *mani* wall is built of stones carved with the mantra *Om Mani Padme Hung.*

As a businessman, sponsoring these devotions seemed to Drilo a good bargain, a relatively easy way to buy his way out of hell. But when my mother told him that he needed to recite the mantra *Om Mani Padme Hung* daily, he balked. "I won't do it. I don't have time." Almost every Tibetan recites this mantra of the lord of compassion, Avalokiteshvara, many times a day, and some very virtuous practitioners go into retreat to recite one hundred and eight million. Drilo stubbornly refused to do even one hundred and eight until another demonstration of my mother's extraordinary abilities changed his mind.

My mother was asked to do seven days of long-life ceremonies for a lama named Tonpa Tulku. At the beginning of the ceremonies, as was customary, an arrow decorated with silk streamers was put on the altar and a piece of string was cut the same length as the arrow. If the length of the arrow increased in the course of the ceremonies, it would be an indication that the length of the lama's life had correspondingly increased. My mother gave Drilo the piece of string and told him to keep it until the conclusion of the ceremonies.

Usually my mother was a perfectionist about every aspect of ritual. There are monks living today who remember occasions when she flung her bell across the room or whacked them on the head with her bone trumpet because they weren't mindful and made a foolish error. However, during these long-life ceremonies she herself seemed distracted. On the last day she actually slept through the morning session, but upon awakening, she told her attendant that she had had a wonderful dream in which a wisdom being had brought a blessing. "Go look on the altar."

He went, but found nothing unusual. Thinking it a very bad sign to come back empty-handed, he gathered up some black mustard seeds. Seeing them, my mother was puzzled and said, "I don't think this is it. Go look again."

This time the attendant found hundreds of small pills sprinkled everywhere. Such pills hold the essence of long-life blessing, and their spontaneous manifestation was regarded as an indisputable sign of the effectiveness of the ceremonies.

My mother then called Drilo and they measured the string he had kept against the arrow on the altar. The length of the arrow had increased by an inch, another sign that the ceremonies had borne fruit.

Drilo's faith in my mother became so strong that he could no longer refuse to say *Om Mani Padme Hung* one hundred and eight times a day. He wouldn't buy a *mala* (rosary) for counting, so he counted the recitations on his fingers. No one ever suspected him of making a mistake and saying one hundred and nine. He did, however, walk around murmuring, "Delog Dawa Drolma Chhen"—"Great Delog Dawa Drolma"—and he became the sponsor of many of her dharma projects, including the construction of a huge and costly prayer wheel filled with the mantra of the deity Vajrasattva.

Throughout her life people came from great distances to receive my mother's blessings as a healer. She melded the compassionate intention of her mind into various substances, most often by blowing into pure water after reciting mantra. The effectiveness of the healing water depended on the sick person's faith and my mother's power to invoke the purification of wisdom and compassion.

9

NOT LONG AFTER my mother returned from her journey as a *delog*, the family decided to make a pilgrimage to Lhasa. This was a major and very expensive undertaking, so my family sponsored an extensive wealth ceremony to help support the journey.

During a wealth ceremony, one invokes wisdom beings to gather and return one's merit—one's positive, virtuous energy—in the form of prosperity. The intention is to offer the wealth generously and thus to contribute to the well-being of others. If one's motives for performing such ceremonies are selfish, one's accumulated merit is simply used up and one can become more impoverished than before.

Dawa Drolma sat in a place of honor at the ceremony. At this time, she was already famous as a *delog* and recognized as a *siddha,* a person of extraordinary spiritual attainment. The young lama who led the ceremonies was Chagdud Tanpai Gyaltsan, the abbot of Chagdud Gonpa and my previous incarnation.

He was twenty-seven years old and famous as a wild *siddha* who drank prodigious amounts of *arak* and on occasion bent heavy iron swords into folds. Chagdud Tanpai Gyaltsan, like the incarnations of Chagdud before him, had an extraordinary realization of the essential insubstantiality and mutability of the phenomenal world.

In recognition of his deep connection with my mother, at the conclusion of the ceremony he gave her a precious reliquary box and told her that their connection would soon come to fruition. Tanpai Gyaltsan died not long after.

After the ceremony, the family left on its pilgrimage, their caravan of yaks and horses loaded with tents, utensils, a year's supply of food and the many offerings for high lamas that would be necessary in Lhasa. Relatives, lamas, monks, servants and herdsmen were all a part of the caravan. Because of the ever-present threat of attack by brigands, my family, like most pilgrims, traveled in the relative safety of large numbers and with armed men.

For many months the caravan of pilgrims wended its way through the high, craggy mountain passes, the long valleys and deep forests that separate Eastern from Central Tibet. Sometimes they stopped at monasteries, but usually theirs was a nomadic existence, with all the pleasures and hardships that involves.

One day as the entourage passed through a valley, my mother suddenly pointed and exclaimed, "Over there is a *terma* that must be revealed now!" The caravan immediately changed direction and traveled until it came to the rock face of a mountain. At my mother's direction, a man struck the rock with one strong blow of a hatchet and a large slab fell off, exposing a *p'hurba*, or ritual dagger, embedded in stone.

This *p'hurba*, like other sacred objects and teachings Tibetans call *termas*—"treasures"—had been hidden in the eighth century by one of the teachers most revered in Tibet, Padmasambhava. In propagating the Buddha's teachings amid the shamanistic society that dominated Tibet at that time, Padmasambhava saw clearly that some teachings would have to wait for a more appropriate time to take root. He concealed them until certain great practitioners such as my mother would reveal them and bring them to fruition. These practitioners became *tertons*, "treasure discoverers."

Instead of seizing the *p'hurba*, my mother turned abruptly to her sister, who out of jealousy had continually disparaged her accomplishments. "You doubt my abilities," she said, "so demonstrate your own now. You pull this *p'hurba* from the stone."

Her sister, too proud to refuse the challenge and risk losing a moment of glory, grasped the *p'hurba*. With a shriek, she released it. Hot as molten iron, it had seared her hand. My mother stepped forward and pulled the *p'hurba* from the stone as easily as a knife from butter. Inside a hole in the center of the *p'hurba* was a scroll inscribed in the secret language of the "sky goers," the wisdom beings known as *dakinis*. The script, indecipherable except to one with profound wisdom, was revealed by my mother.

At last the caravan crossed the high, semi-arid plateau where Lhasa is situated. Inside the city the family made pilgrimages to the Potala Palace, the Jokhang and numerous other holy places. They visited the high lamas who lived in Lhasa at the time, including Jigdral Yeshe Dorje, Dudjom Rinpoche, the future head of the Nyingmapa tradition of Tibetan Buddhism.

During her stay in Lhasa, my mother established a connection with a very high lama of the Gelugpa tradition, Sera Kharto Tulku. He had been a *terton* in his previous life, and was now a very powerful meditator and the abbot of a monastery near Lhasa. There were many prophecies about him in the texts of Padmasambhava. One stated that when he and his closest friend encountered imprisonment or untimely death, Tibet would soon fall.

Many years later, unfortunately, this prophecy was fulfilled. Kharto Tulku's closest friend, a lama known throughout Tibet, became inadvertently ensnared in a political intrigue and was assassinated. Kharto Tulku was imprisoned for two years because of his friendship with this lama, and died shortly after his release. At the moment of his death, he stood up, took the threatening posture of a wrathful deity and held that pose for two weeks. Exactly as the prophecy had foretold, the circumstances of Kharto Tulku's imprisonment and his friend's death signaled disintegration in Tibet, which would leave the country vulnerable to the Chinese takeover.

Although in the Gelugpa tradition it is not permissible for lamas to marry, secret trysts are not unheard of. Near the end of my mother's stay in Lhasa, she conceived a child by Kharto Tulku. The two did not marry. Instead she returned to Tromt'har with her family. Three years had passed since they left.

Soon after, a sealed letter arrived for my mother from Dzogchhen Rinpoche, a lama respected throughout Tibet. He wrote, "In your womb there is a great *tulku* who will be known as T'hubtan Geleg Palzang. Take special care, keep very clean and eat only the purest food for the full term of your pregnancy."

Tulku is a word with many levels of meaning in Tibetan, but usually it refers to a being of extraordinary spiritual attainment who has intentionally taken a specific rebirth in order to benefit others. Before birth the *tulku* directs his or her consciousness toward the union of specific parents so that the circumstances of birth and upbringing will be an auspicious beginning for spiritual activity.

A second letter arrived from Kharto Tulku, which accurately foretold many events in the life of his child in my mother's womb. My mother took these letters to heart and was very careful during her pregnancy. I was born in the Iron Horse Year, 1930, on a mountaintop named T'hurgan Lhakhang—"Abode of the Gods."

2

Tulku

DESPITE my being a *tulku*—or perhaps because of it—I was a terror as a child. Tibetans sometimes say that *tulkus* are wild and willful as children, but that this same energy propels them toward spiritual accomplishment if it is properly harnessed. To this high purpose, Tibetans spare no effort with the rod. My mother and I lived in Tromt'har until I was three. I retain wisps of pleasurable childhood memories—nestling inside my mother's sheepskin coat and holding on to her back as we rode on a horse; watching my grandmother's servants churning milk into butter by shaking it in a yak skin; my beautiful auntie with her pink cheeks, turquoise ornaments and belt made of pierced silver coins—but these memories are as tenuous as a half-remembered dream.

More tenacious and vivid are the memories of my childhood dramas of sorrow and conflict, the incidents that were grist for my development and training. Tibet is in the flyway of migrating birds, and in the fall countless varieties flocked in the meadows there. Fascinated, I wanted to capture one and keep it for a pet. The older children told me how a bird could be trapped, and with this method in mind, I set out with a basket, a stick, a bit of string and a handful of barley. After many failed attempts, I finally trapped a swallow under the basket. I reached in carefully and caught it in my hand. Stroking its feathers delighted me, and I coached it to eat a few kernels of grain. When I showed the adults my new pet, however, their reaction spoiled my pleasure.

"You must let it go, T'hubga. A wild bird won't survive unless it can fly free. It isn't like a dog or a lamb. You can't make it a pet." Their admonishments only provoked my fierce will. I loved my little bird. It was mine and I would care for it; their words couldn't wrest it from me. Instead of releasing it, I slipped it into my *chuba,* the wraparound robe that Tibetans wear as an outer garment. That night before I fell asleep, I cradled my cherished pet in my hand one more time and gently tucked it back into my *chuba.* In the morning it was dead. I cried bitterly, inconsolably. This was the first great loss I ever experienced.

I was always very protective of children smaller or younger than I, though I would take on anyone else. This meant I was frequently engaged in battles. One day my maternal grandmother intervened in a fight between me and another child, and pinioned my arms. "Now all of you teach him not to fight!" she commanded. She held me as five or six children jumped on me, pummeling me with their fists. Sobbing and furious, I felt as if I would suffocate under the pile. Suddenly I found my hand on my little knife. Yanking it from its sheath, I stabbed blindly. One of my cousins, an older girl, emitted a piercing scream. The children scrambled off me and stared in stunned silence as my cousin, wailing in pain and indignation, revealed her wound. Since she, like all of us, wore a tough sheepskin *chuba,* my knife thrust had not done much damage. Still, it had punctured her side and caused enough bleeding that everyone was shocked. The children would never play with me again, and made a game of scattering and shouting fearfully whenever I approached. I became very lonely, but in the immediate aftermath of the stabbing, I was sullen and truculent, as I fully expected an unmerciful beating.

The beating never came, probably because of the intervention of the girl's mother, my beautiful auntie, who was always gentle and calm. My own mother must not have been home, because I cannot imagine her allowing me to go unpunished. There were days when she would beat me not once, but three or four times. Each time my anger would escalate, I would yell more abusively, and when she released me, I would repeat whatever I had been doing wrong with more fervor. It was an immense and exhausting clash of wills, but in her compassion my mother could not let me grow up wild and ungovernable. Although eventually I would experience deep regret that I had inflicted so much trouble on my mother, so much suffering on one who was an emanation of Tara, there was no residue of bitterness between us. Sometimes, as soon as she had punished me, we would embrace and the conflict would dissolve. For my grandmother, though, I harbored a grudge that lasted for almost two decades. Its origin was not in her setting me up to be trounced by the other children, but in her not sharing evenhandedly a little nub of sausage.

One day I and several other children were in our family tent while my grandmother was eating a large link sausage. At the end of it was a balloon where the sausage casing had expanded in the hot fat. Each child coveted this end piece, and each begged for it. "Please, Amala, please give it to me!"

"No! To me!"

"To me! To me!"

"Please, Amala . . ."

The innocence and single-mindedness of our desire made us extremely vulnerable to her decision, and when my grandmother gave the balloon to her favorite child, perhaps each of the other children felt as I did—deprived and unloved. I proceeded to make myself more unlovable by saying terrible things to her and later, when my mother and I lived in a different region, by stationing myself by the road and throwing rocks at her horse as she arrived to visit with my mother.

The special affection children usually feel for their grandparents I reserved for my great aunt. She was a wonderful meditator who seldom lay down to sleep. I would come and nestle against her, and as she murmured her mantras, I would drift off in her lap. She radiated warmth, peace and the deep comfort I longed for as I chafed against the obstacles in my childish mind. When dinner was brought to us, I fed her from my bowl and she fed me from hers, and she would stroke my head.

WHEN I WAS three years old, a delegation of monks from Chagdud Gonpa arrived in Tromt'har to search for the reincarnation of Tanpai Gyaltsan, the previous Chagdud Tulku. They had consulted a number of high lamas, who had indicated that his incarnation had been born in the Tromge clan as the son of Dawa Drolma.

In addition, there had been the monk from Chagdud Gonpa who had witnessed the singular exchange between Dawa Drolma and Tanpai Gyaltsan and the gift of the reliquary. Thus, when the delegation arrived, there was little doubt about where to look for the child; the suspense lay in whether the child—that is, whether I—could pass rigorous tests verifying that I was the incarnation, the *tulku*, of the abbot of Chagdud Gonpa. Without hesitation I identified the objects that had been Tanpai Gyaltsan's, and when a monk who had been close to Tanpai Gyaltsan came in, I greeted him by name. Nevertheless, a dilemma arose, because my mother was not home and my grandfather had to receive the delegation and accept the recognition that I was Chagdud Tulku. Not to accept, according to Tibetan custom, might create obstacles to the fulfillment of my life's purpose. To accept, however, traditionally meant that I would be returned to my monastery to be trained. My grandfather took the middle course. He accepted a set of monk's clothes, but he made no agreement about my return to Chagdud Gonpa.

My Tromge relatives rejoiced in my being formally recognized as Chagdud Tulku, and although there may have been those among them who looked forward to my being sent away to the monastery, they thought my grandfather had been adroit in his handling of the situation. Everyone was amazed, therefore, when my mother returned home and became enraged when she was told what had occurred. She berated her father fiercely. "Are you tired of feeding my son and me? Are you tired of providing our clothes? Or is it that your home has become too small for us? Never mind, for soon you will be free of us."

She began making preparations to leave. My grandfather, a fine, vital man, had no means to counter her arguments because in any ordinary sense they were irrational. He came to me with tears in his eyes. "You always have a home with me," he said, "and you needn't worry about food and clothing as long as I have anything at all." I knew what he said was true, and I loved him very much.

To say my mother's behavior was inexplicable and irrational is not to say it was egotistical or wrong. Her awareness was beyond the limitations of time, space and apparent circumstances, and her actions arose spontaneously from wisdom. Later the family would understand that it was necessary for her to leave them in order to fulfill an aspect of her destiny that had been prophesied long before, that she should stabilize the health and life of Tulku Gyurmed Namchag Dorje, a very old, frail lama who was the abbot of Tenp'hel Gonpa. This had been foretold by Padmasambhava himself. Whatever else necessitated her furious stance in regard to my recognition as a *tulku,* her break with Tromt'har and her move to Tenp'hel Gonpa cannot be ascertained now, more than fifty years later. Perhaps by exiting from the center of fiery conflict she caused her father less heartache; perhaps the conflict arose from the need to protect me. My grandfather visited us at Tenp'hel Gonpa soon after we moved there, and my mother and he were completely reconciled.

For me the move to Tenp'hel Gonpa, about a week away on horseback, marked the beginning of my formal training as a lama. For the next seven years, until I went into three-year retreat at the age of eleven, my life would alternate between periods of strict discipline in which my every move would be under the surveillance of my tutors and interludes in which my suppressed energy would explode. Throughout, I had many visions, many clairvoyant experiences, many extraordinary dreams, and within these, I sometimes had glimpses of absolute open awareness. My mother and my teachers took note of these as indications of special abilities I had developed in previous lifetimes, but they never wavered from their intention that I should go through the rigors of Buddhist training in this lifetime, or from their certainty that only through effort would I reestablish the effortless realization I had attained previously.

IN THE DREAM I was playing inside the stone fence of my mother's front yard. A dog came and slowly transformed into a deer. The deer transformed into a lama, and the lama into a dragon. Wondrously, I beheld the dragon as it rose, took flight and disappeared into the clouds. I could hear its roar echoing in the vault of the sky. When I asked a lama, he said, "I think it was a dream about your own life, which you have begun as a very naughty child."

TENP'HEL GONPA is northeast of Tromt'har, on the other side of a towering mountain range. It is in the region of the kingdom of Gesar, the epic warrior of Tibet, and it is clear why Gesar saw this land, with its rolling hills, grassy meadows and sparkling rivers, as well worth winning and defending. The elevation is more than twelve thousand feet, but the landscape is gentle and expansive.

Tenp'hel Gonpa itself was a monastery surrounded by a complex of houses for the monks. This monastic community was situated along a river, and nomads often set up camp on the other side. Sometimes they came to graze their herds; at other times they gathered for an event at the monastery. There were a number of other monasteries in the region, the nearest an hour away on horseback. News traveled rapidly and was traded like currency, the most sought after being anecdotes about the lamas. My mother's house was beautifully located on a high bluff overlooking a valley that forked into the valley of Tenp'hel Gonpa, and was about a half hour's walk away from the monastery.

One day, when I was about four, a nun arrived at the door. She had made the long journey from Lhasa at the request of my father, Sera Kharto Tulku, and she was there to teach me how to meditate. She gave me no instructions regarding what to contemplate or how to hold my mind, but she was an expert in enforcing proper meditation posture. She made me sit with my back absolutely straight and rigid, my legs crossed and my feet resting soles-up on my thighs, my hands on my knees, my chin tucked in and my tongue curled back to the roof of my mouth. Some days she made me close my eyes, and if I opened them, she thumped me on the forehead and said, "Meditate." Some days my eyes had to be open in an immovable gaze. If I dozed, she thumped me. "Meditate." This went on from the moment I awoke until bedtime, for weeks or perhaps months. In the excruciating pain and boredom, I lost track of time. There were no breaks; our meals were brought to us. My only reprieve was to go out to urinate, so I went many times a day. When the nun saw I was abusing this privilege, she refused to let me go at all. There were accidents and she beat me for disgracing myself.

One day it was absolutely necessary for me to go out. Knowing what the nun's answer would be if I asked permission, I simply jumped up and ran past her. She lashed out at me with her *mala,* which was made of very large, hard beads. They cracked against my shaven monk's head and raised a series of bumps. Blinded by pain and tears, I ran to the arms of my mother and sobbed uncontrollably. After comforting me, my mother summoned the nun. "This is my only son," she said. "Perhaps he does not learn well, but surely his life should not be taken. At least while he has life, there is hope." Then she sent the nun away.

SOON AFTER the nun's departure, my mother went to the family treasurer and requested that he sit with me each day. Lama Tse Gon's tactics for training me were completely different from the nun's. If I learned to read certain lines or memorize certain passages, he allowed me to play for a short time. I usually could not go out and play with other children, but I could put my books down and play for a while near him. Even this was an incentive to accomplish my studies quickly. When I studied especially well, he rewarded me with little toys he made himself. With a scrap of cloth, a bit of wood and some string, he fashioned a tiny tent held up by posts, lines and stakes. He carved toy people and miniature animals, and he taught me how to carve. He had a very good hand, and he was a source of my artistic ability in later years. During this time I had a recurring dream of a pot of melted butter cooking together with freshly pounded quartz dust and of myself eating this slightly gritty mixture quite naturally. Lama Tse Gon thought the dream meant that I was beginning to digest what I was reading. I responded to Lama Tse Gon's kindness and warmth, and over time I came to consider him as my *gegan*, the teacher with whom I had a true bond. Affectionately I called him *gegan-la*.

I WAS VERY SICK, and for five days I had been in bed, vomiting and enduring a severe headache. That fifth night, as I lay in a state between waking and sleeping, a vision swirled before me in the vortex of a huge tornado. Monstrous, it had the body of a human and the head of a bird. In one hand, it held a lasso of intestines; in the other, an enormous, bloated stomach that it hurled like a lightning bolt. Then it swirled away, casting a last glance at me over its shoulder. Immediately a woman came, calling me, "Son! Son! Take care!" She had a pale blue complexion, very long blue hair that hung almost to her feet, and she rode a dancing blue lion. Flowers were strewn all around her. She handed me a bow and arrow and said, "O Son! Now do it well!"

The stomach exuded a violet stream that resembled incense smoke. This smoke wafted over two persons from our area, a monk named Norgay and a young woman named Yungdrung. As I took the bow and arrow, a song arose spontaneously to my lips:

> I draw the bow of the unborn, free of elaboration.
> I pull back the arrow of unceasing, inherent great-minded
>   compassion.
> I send it forth with the power of unhindered enlightened
>   activity.
> I hit the target of those without realization who lead
>   astray.

At that moment, I shot the arrow directly into the stomach. It flew with the sound of "*Hung!*" which resonated like the roar of a dragon. Flames engulfed the stomach until nothing remained.

Lama Tse Gon lay in his bed beside mine. His expression was grave when I described all that had happened. "You have no understanding of these things, nor have you ever heard words like these. This experience shows that you have a strong habit from past lives that carries over into this life. It also indicates that you are being protected and will recover from your sickness, and because you destroyed the stomach, which is a bag of disease, our region will not be subject to an epidemic. However, those two persons who were touched by the smoke may fall ill. Say nothing about this, for if you speak of it, obstacles to your life could arise. If you keep it secret, your visionary powers will grow stronger and clearer."

I took all he said to heart and never chattered about my visionary experiences. As Lama Tse Gon predicted, they became more frequent and more lucid, until now not ten days pass without my having such an experience.

Also as Lama Tse Gon foresaw, the monk Norgay and the woman Yungdrung became ill and died soon after.

IT WAS TIME for me to receive an empowerment and to do Manjushri practice. The deity Manjushri is the full, spontaneous expression of all qualities of intelligence and transcendent knowledge, and Manjushri practice removes obstacles to learning. A high lama, Khanpo Ngagwang Nyandrag, gave me the empowerment and teachings for Manjushri meditation and prepared me for a fourteen-day Manjushri retreat, which would be my first retreat. During those two weeks I could not eat certain substances such as meat, onions and garlic. With deep faith, I began practice by invoking the blessings of the wisdom beings and praying that my own qualities of intelligence and wisdom would come to full fruition. These are the spontaneous qualities of mind's true nature, but they are obscured by the habits and delusion of the egocentric mind.

24

Lama Tse Gon helped me set up a shrine, and we placed on it a beautiful little cup with a pill made of special substances that were to be saturated with the blessings of Manjushri through my practice. The signs were very good. I had a dream about finding a long sword—the sword that cuts off dualistic concepts—as well as several direct visions of Manjushri. Throughout the seven days of meditation the blessings of Manjushri were absorbed into the pill, empowering it. I swallowed it on the seventh day. That day I visited the *khanpo*. Whenever I went to see him, he gave me a little treat, such as a piece of rock candy, dried fruit or meat jerky. As he was rummaging around looking for something to give me, he said, "I don't have any candy today, and I can't give you meat because of your Manjushri practice. What should I give you?"

"Oh," I lied, "I already ate meat today."

He was surprised. "You are not supposed to have meat until you complete the practice seven days from now."

"I did have meat today, though."

"Well, I guess if you are not keeping that commitment it is all right if you have some more." He sliced a piece off his slab of dried meat and I ate it.

A few days later the *khanpo* came to visit Lama Tse Gon and they discussed my practice. Both were pleased with my signs, but the *khanpo* remarked to Lama Tse Gon, "You know, he's not supposed to be eating any meat." It was Lama Tse Gon's turn to be surprised. "Of course, not! What makes you think he is eating meat?"

The *khanpo* and Lama Tse Gon both looked at me. I tried to avoid their gaze. Then we all laughed. I had fibbed and they had caught me, but they didn't punish me.

LAMA TSE GON began to incorporate formal meditation practice into my daily schedule. After he awakened me in the morning, we would do some Manjushri practice, and he taught me to use a bell and small hand drum. I would study all day; then in the evening we would do a practice to invoke the blessings of the dharma protectors, those who safeguard practitioners on the path to enlightenment by shielding them from nonvirtue. Lama Tse Gon taught me how to use cymbals and a large drum in connection with this practice. His informal teachings during the same period were quite wonderful. Once, when he heard that I and the other children had been teasing an old beggar woman who often harassed us, he admonished me, "It is acceptable to confront those who are your equals if they mistreat you, but if you are abused by those of low stature, it is improper to strike back. They are caught in degraded circumstances because they have not generated virtue in the past, and actually they are quite powerless. Their predicament is cause for compassion. You undermine your own noble mind if you are aggressive toward or mistreat them in any way, no matter what they have done to you." His words made me recognize my wrongdoing, and I left the beggar woman alone.

WE WERE SITTING on the porch, Lama Tse Gon, the *khanpo*, several monks and I. Lama Tse Gon was sewing, as he often did for my mother and me because he was an excellent tailor. Unexpectedly, I saw his brother riding up on a horse. The horse suddenly stumbled, and both rider and horse crashed to the ground. I jumped up, threw out my arms and shouted, "Oh, no! They have fallen!"

"What's wrong?" Lama Tse Gon asked. I realized then that the scene I had witnessed had taken place only in my mind's eye. I described it, but thought I had been confused.

A couple of hours later Lama Tse Gon's brother actually did ride up. Lama Tse Gon asked him how his journey had been, and he replied, "A little difficult. My horse stepped in a hole and we both fell." My clairvoyant abilities were not reliable, however. Usually when people came and asked me questions, I did not see anything. I couldn't see on demand; I saw spontaneously when something broke through my ordinary consciousness.

LAMA TSE GON had to leave for some months to perform death ceremonies for my mother's herdsman. Suddenly released from strict discipline and constant supervision, I created general havoc, then capped it off with one of the blackest incidents of my childhood.

Most people were either tolerant of or carefully patient with me, mainly out of respect for my mother but also for me as a *tulku* who occasionally displayed extraordinary abilities. There were, however, exceptions to this forbearance. My mother, for example, beat me almost daily, and her friend Bidema lodged complaint after complaint with my mother each time she saw me doing anything wrong.

During this time my mother had a servant named Tashi who was thirteen years old and helped with the cooking. She always gave me the skim off the boiled milk, and she played with me and told stories whenever she had time. Though she knew only three or four stories, she told them well and I loved hearing them again and again. Tashi was also a bit of a thief. My mother was not careful about picking up the offerings people gave her, so Tashi pocketed some of them. She took enough to be noticed but not to worry about, and certainly I never reported her, any more than she reported my misdeeds. In our unspoken complicity, we got along very well.

One day I was tossing stones off the rock outcrop in my mother's yard. Some visitors were coming up the road below, and a rock almost hit one of them. I had not seen the visitors so this was an accident, but Bidema had seen me and assumed I was up to my usual mischief. She went straight to my mother, who was furious and who struck me again and again.

I was furious, too, full of righteous indignation at being, for once, falsely accused. As soon as my mother released me, I went storming to Bidema's tent and flung open the tent flaps. No one was there. A pale shaft of light from the smoke hole illuminated a clay pot on the fire containing boiling sweet potato soup. A mortar and pestle were next to the stove. Without pausing to think, I picked up the pestle and smashed the pot. Soup, shards, steam and ashes exploded. I threw the pestle into the rubble and fled, brushing off the ashes that had dusted me like snow.

In the safety of my own yard, I resumed my play guiltlessly, and this is how my mother found me. She was a manifestation of total wrath as she jerked me up and began to shake and whip me with a small riding crop. Bidema came out of our house to scold me and goad my mother; her rage and frustration knew no bounds, and she wept as she made bitter denunciations. My own anger welled up and suddenly the word "thief" sprang to my lips. Bidema immediately protested, but I continued relentlessly. "Thief! Thief! Where is the coral bead you took from my mother? Where is the silver clasp?" Item by item I named the things I had seen Tashi pocket. The more vehemently Bidema protested, the more firmly I persevered in my lie.

At first my mother didn't believe me and threatened to whip me yet again, but then she stopped and let me go. I don't think I convinced her and certainly she didn't turn against Bidema even slightly. Probably the whole incident could have been dropped right there in our yard except that Bidema took her grievances against me to other people, and some of them gave credence to my accusation. This damaged her reputation and eventually she moved away.

I was delighted. I should have been remorseful over the trouble my lying tongue brought her, but instead I was glad to be free of the trouble her tattling tongue brought me. Nevertheless, I did not escape the karmic repercussions of my false accusations. In later life there would be times when others would accuse me—falsely, but perhaps not unjustly.

MY BELOVED *gegan-la,* Lama Tse Gon, had still not returned from his journey, and my mother's patience with my wild, unruly behavior was finished. She decided my vacation should be terminated and my training should resume immediately, despite Lama Tse Gon's absence. To supervise my training she selected one of the most formidable lamas in the Tenp'hel Gonpa region, Lama Wanga.

The word *wang* means "powerful," and Lama Wanga lived up to his name. If monks and lamas were engaged in casual conversation and someone happened to see him coming, those who could slipped away, and the rest stopped their chatter and sat very still and straight until he passed by. He said nothing to them, but his scowl seemed to activate their consciences. Sitting in the same room with him made people nervous and uncomfortable. He never joked, rarely smiled and never violated his own strict discipline.

My mother arranged for a monk to accompany me to Lama Wanga's house, loaded with an enormous leg of dried yak meat, a large bag of *tsampa* and a big ball of butter. Wanga lived about half a mile away, between my mother's house and Tenp'hel Gonpa. His house was very small, a retreat hut really, with room for his bed, a shrine, a tiny kitchen and storage. A little bed was made for me by the shrine.

From the first day I was integrated into Lama Wanga's schedule. At the first crow of the rooster, he sat up, lit a butterlamp and began his practice. At dawn he woke me up and I recited Manjushri mantra, counting the beads of my *mala*. Then his sister, who was a nun, brought us tea, butter and *tsampa*. We didn't get up to eat; everything was brought to us.

Between breakfast and lunch I read my assigned texts aloud to him. He recited his mantra continuously and kept his prayer wheel revolving, but his ear was open and he detected the slightest mistake. If I made two or three in a row, he said in a heavy tone, "Your teacher has been lax. You are making too many mistakes." Then he reached over and pinched me hard on the thigh. A bruise would be evident several days later. Beyond that he applied no other discipline, but the menacing possibility was unmistakable.

I was not allowed to play, but I could go out to relieve myself as necessary. I could walk, I didn't have to run out and back, but I didn't test the repercussions of dallying.

Visitors came by occasionally, but Lama Wanga wasn't hospitable. He greeted them and answered their questions, and they left. In this respect Lama Wanga was the opposite of Lama Tse Gon, who enjoyed company and conversation. When people came to my mother's house, Lama Tse Gon didn't want me sing-songing the alphabet in the background, so he would send me out to play, sometimes for an hour or two until the visit was over.

Each afternoon Lama Wanga rolled up his little carpet, tucked it under his arm and walked with me to a high meadow. When we reached our spot, he unrolled the carpet for me to sit on while he sat on the ground. The view overlooked the monastery, and it seemed we could gaze out across the whole world. We never chatted, but instead sustained an unbroken chain of *mantra* recitation, accompanied by the monotonous click-click of his prayer wheel revolving. In the evening we would be served more *tsampa* and tea, and then we would continue to sit and practice until bedtime. Day after day passed—for three months—with no interruption in this routine. I longed for the return of Lama Tse Gon, my affectionate *gegan-la,* and the relative freedom he gave me. I had derived indisputable benefit from my stay with Lama Wanga, however. My reading had improved more in three months with him than it had in two years with Lama Tse Gon and I had experienced an extended period of disciplined practice.

IN THE DREAM I was playing on an island with five or six other children when the ground began to tremble and boil. This turbulent soil suddenly broke open and revealed a huge snakelike animal with a massive head and bulging eyes that glared straight at me. It swayed before me, hideous beyond belief, infected with oozing, bleeding sores.

My first reaction was overwhelming fear, but when I saw

the creature's anguish, my fear melted into compassion. Awareness of its suffering lifted me off the ground into flight. A vase appeared in my hand, and from it I poured orange nectar over the animal's body, flooding the surface. The relief of the creature, a kind of supernatural animal called *naga,* was immediate.

A sense of subtle pride rippled through me as I surveyed the benefit I had accomplished for the *naga.* Instantaneously, steam sprayed from it and condensed on my body, just as if I had broken out in a feverish sweat. My whole body felt numb, and as this feeling increased, all I could think to do was call out to my mother, "Ama! Ama!" Out of the sky riding a white vulture came a woman holding a mirror. She looked like a beautiful Tibetan woman with jet black hair, white skin and rosy cheeks and lips. She wore a red skirt, flowers were entwined in her crown and her body was adorned with garland necklaces, bracelets and anklets. As the vulture swooped toward me, the woman held up the mirror and offered me an omniscient view of the whole universe. A dazzling array of prophetic events passed before my eyes. A vision of a cremation foreshadowed the cremation of my mother five years later. All kinds of strange animals, moving in odd, inexplicable ways, I would recognize decades later as cars, cranes and heavy machinery, which were unknown in Tibet in the 1930s. I saw many other things, but I could not understand their meaning as prophecies. Then the woman spoke to me:

Excellent, how excellent!
The black naga demon below
and the small boy with love and compassion—
how excellent is this unpremeditated intention.
The meadows, trees and flowers below
and the fine, sweet rain from on high—

how excellent is this unpremeditated intention.
The blessings of the Three Jewels on high
and the faith and samaya of those below—
how excellent is this unpremeditated intention.
Images of joy and sorrow,
movements of the dance, adroitly shifting—
see these as teachers of impermanence, of illusion . . .

Saying this, the woman disappeared and the dream ended. When I related these dreams to Lama Tse Gon, he made a list of them and said, "It seems that you are troubled by some slight harm from nagas. The omens that arose in the mirror indicate that you would be free of these obstacles if you undertook intensive retreats on Tara, Hayagriva and Vajra-kilaya. It also seems that you will not stay for long in any one place. Even if I live a long life, I probably will not see you in my old age." At this, he looked sad.

DURING MY CHILDHOOD there was so little time to be with my mother, and so much of the time we had together was spent in stormy conflicts of will. For this reason there is a profound tenderness in my recollection of certain simple moments we shared. I remember her chopping some meat, frying it in butter and giving it to me. This fragile, intimate moment is suspended timelessly in my memory.

3

The Archer

I HAD BEEN PLAYING alone on the rock outcrop in my mother's yard, and on impulse I decided to meditate. I had just turned four and had received no real meditation training—I knew only how to sit in correct posture, so that is what I did. Suddenly a yogi appeared in front of me. His hair was tied in a topknot and was as white as snow. His moustache and wispy beard were also white and stood out against his skin, which was deep nut brown. He wore a white cloth draped around him and over one shoulder. In his right hand he held a *chod* drum and in his left a bell, and he chanted in verse:

> Cut through concepts woven from dualistic appearances:
> *A Ah!*
> Abide in the citadel of self-arising awareness: *A Ah!*
> Waver not from the unceasing energy of awareness: *A Ah!*
> Like child's play, there is nothing to abandon,
> nothing to grasp! *A Ah!*

He continued the above refrain, reciting many other stanzas, now forgotten. When he finished, he disappeared as naturally as mist dissipates into sunshine. I continued to sit, conceptless, in open awareness, after he had gone.

I went to tell my mother, who was visiting with a friend, an elderly monk named Lama Atse. I described my vision and repeated the verses I had heard. At that time I could remember almost all of them. My mother was very quiet, and Lama Atse spoke. "You saw the great *siddha* and father of the practice of *chod,* P'hadampa Sangye. His verses were a direct introduction to the nature of your own mind and a prophecy about your life." Both my mother and he cautioned me not to talk about it.

Sometime later Lama Atse gave me an empowerment and my first teachings on the practice of *chod.* In the following years I listened to other *chod* teachings from other teachers as well, and each time I heard them I explored new depths in the fathomless meaning of this practice, which cultivates supreme generosity. The practitioner cuts attachment and self-clinging at the very root in the mind and fearlessly makes a vast offering of everything, even his or her body itself, to whomever would partake of it, helpers and harmdoers alike. In the case of harmdoers, the aspiration of the *chod* practitioner is that they will be so satisfied by the offering that they will refrain from inflicting harm and will turn their minds toward virtue. Thus, *chod* is a healing practice that can benefit those who are afflicted by negative forces, either the inner forces of sickness and mental turmoil, or the outer ones of injurious and demonic beings. The suffering of the afflicted persons and the afflictive entities is dispersed simultaneously.

When I was about eight years old, some people came from a village fifteen miles away and requested that my mother return with them to perform a *chod* ceremony. There was a terrible epidemic in their area, probably anthrax, though they did not name it. Their animals became infected with open sores and their livers became horribly diseased. If humans touched the blood of an infected animal, they too fell ill. A number of persons had died and the herds were endangered. Because my mother could not leave at that time, she suggested they take me instead. "Have faith," she assured them. "The result will be just as if I were there."

I rode away with the villagers and nine good practitioners, including Lama Tse Gon and Lama Atse. This was the first time I was to be the *vajra* master, the presiding lama. I sat on the highest throne and was responsible for the conduct of the ceremony. Outwardly this meant that I needed to know the elaborate songs of *chod* in sequence and to accompany myself with bell, drum and *kangling,* a thighbone trumpet. Inwardly it meant that the success of the ceremony depended to a large extent on the power of my beneficial intention, my visualization and my ability to accomplish the offering through meditation. For three days we did extensive practice. In one section a practitioner takes the pose of P'hadampa Sangye and sings praises. Lama Atse stopped the ceremony and said I should do this section. My expression and stance of mind were so evocative of P'hadampa Sangye that tears of faith flooded Lama Atse's eyes. Soon after, the epidemic ceased.

ABOUT THE SAME TIME as he taught me *chod,* Lama Atse taught me *p'howa,* transference of consciousness. This practice is done at the moment of death or soon after to transfer the dead person's consciousness from the *bardo*—the intermediate state between one birth and another—to a realm of pure awareness such as the pureland of the Buddha Amitabha. There is no suffering in the purelands, and beings are able to accomplish the path to full enlightenment blissfully, without obstacles. If transference cannot be made to a pureland, then at least it can be used to avert great suffering and to direct rebirth as a well-born human or in other high realms of existence. Tibetans rely on their lamas to do *p'howa* for their deceased relatives, and when a family member dies, many offerings are made to generate merit and ensure that transference is accomplished. Actually, *p'howa* is a relatively easy practice to learn and accomplish for oneself, but requires considerable power and skill to accomplish for someone else. In training me, Lama Atse stressed strong visualization, but he emphasized pure motivation more. "Think of the dead person. Remember that he has lost everything he held dear including his own body, that he is being blown about helplessly with no place to sit, no food to eat and no one to rely on but you to release him from the turbulence of the *bardo* or the possibility of a difficult rebirth.

"Think about the relatives who have lost their loved one. What they can do is very limited. Their hope is in you. Meditate from the depth of your love and compassion, and concentrate on the accomplishment of transference. Otherwise you will fail the dead, you will fail the living and you will fail yourself by breaking your commitment to them."

NOW THE FOCUS of Lama Tse Gon's guidance shifted from simply teaching me to read and write to establishing a firm foundation for understanding the Buddha's teachings. I received empowerments for many deity practices, including those of Chakrasamvara, Vajra Yogini and Wrathful Guru

Rinpoche. From my mother I received a treasure of long-life practice.

I received one of my practices in a rather unusual way. One day Lama Tse Gon and I walked to a place near Tenp'hel Gonpa where there was a repository for *satsas,* small molded images that Tibetans make as a devotional activity, and for miscellaneous pages of dharma texts. Tibetan texts consist of rectangular pages held unbound between two hard covers, and sometimes a few pages are misplaced. Since Tibetans regard even a single word of the dharma—the precious Buddhist teachings—as sacred and worthy of respect, they deposit odd pages in a special place.

When we arrived, we found that the glorious late spring weather had prompted others to stroll there, too. Lama Tse Gon joined the monks and villagers who had clustered, chatting and joking, amid the meadow grasses and flowers. I joined the children who were climbing on the repository and playing with the *satsas*. One page of a text fell out from among the *satsas* and drifted to the ground. Suddenly a man appeared in very odd garb. He wore an outer robe, but not like a monk's robe or a lay person's *chuba,* and he wore a huge, peculiar, wide-brimmed hat. No one in our region dressed in this fashion. He looked at me and said, "Nyima Odzer!" I didn't respond at first because I had forgotten Nyima Odzer was one of my names. Tibetans often have more than one name because it is customary to receive a new dharma name when one takes an empowerment from a great lama.

"Nyima Odzer! This is yours!" He picked up the page of text that had fallen to the ground and handed it to me. It was a very short practice of the meditational deity Hayagriva. Then he left. The other children and I went over to the adults, and one of the children asked, "Who was that man in the big black hat?" None of the adults had seen him, but all the children had. Everyone thought this was strange because in such an open place comings and goings were easily observed. Then I showed them the page of text the man had handed me. "Perhaps this is a sign that you should do this practice," Lama Tse Gon said. I wasn't able to get the empowerment immediately, but eventually I did and the practice became very important to me.

LAMA TSE GON became the instructor of a three-year retreat being conducted by several lamas and monks at Tenp'hel Gonpa when I was eight. I accompanied him and listened as he taught the preliminary practices. For almost everyone the path of Tibetan Vajrayana Buddhism begins with four contemplations: the preciousness of human birth as a vehicle for spiritual attainment; impermanence and death; the karmic law of cause and effect; the pervasiveness of suffering for all beings trapped in realms of existence conditioned by delusion, attachment and aversion. I contemplated each of these four reflections very deeply, but the contemplation of impermanence and death brought about the most profound changes in my mind. I observed the play of phenomena so closely that in the end I actually saw that they had no stability, no solidity, no immutable core. I experienced the dreamlike quality of everything. I could penetrate a boulder or a building or a piece of iron with my understanding and directly know that their components had come together, had coalesced and would fall into dissolution. Nothing holds together forever. Full realization of the nature of impermanence thoroughly undercuts attachment. My realization wasn't as complete as this. Still, I ceased to rely deeply on the apparent truth of the ordinary phenomenal world.

THE OLD BARD was blind and legless, but when he sang the epic songs of Gesar, we lived inside his stories. He could sing them for a month and never repeat himself. We revered Gesar himself, the ultimate warrior whose battles won him a fair share of Central Asia, whose spiritual skills brought liberation to companions and enemies alike. We laughed at Gesar's crafty uncle, playing the role of a thwarted buffoon to provide grist for Gesar's development. We followed each point of diplomatic negotiation and each battle as if it were a compelling event in which we ourselves were engaged. Since the Tenp'hel Gonpa region was in the heart of Gesar's kingdom, for me the stories made the land come alive with the pounding hooves of splendid horses and the pageantry of brave warriors.

The Gesar stories fueled my love of weapons. I had a bow and arrow, and I was an accurate archer if the target was inanimate. I wasn't above aiming at animals, but because I could not bear to look at them when I shot, I was fortunate never to hit one. I did, however, take unflinching aim at and fully intended to kill one human being, my mother's consort— my stepfather Sodga. He was extremely handsome, quite affable, unfailingly kind to me and a great realization holder who throughout his life demonstrated excellent practice. I found his presence unbearable, an intrusion on my fierce bond with my mother. It was the catalyst that caused my mind's poisons to brew into a violent explosion. The issue I fixed on was his tying up a bag of treats.

When people came to visit my mother, they often brought her gifts of dried fruits, candies, dried cheese and fried pastries. Some of the prized candies came from China. My mother put everything in a bag and I had free access to these treats. After Sodga arrived, he tied up the bag. He didn't deny me anything I wanted from it, but I had to ask first because he used the treats in his practice as offerings to a mandala of deities. However, his generosity made little impression on me at the time. I saw the tie on the treat bag and I planned to kill him.

One day as he was sitting by a window, the back of his head just visible above the sill, I aimed an arrow and shot at his shaven dome. Then I ran for my life. About a hundred yards away I looked back. Instead of a collapsed body, I saw my stepfather doubled over laughing. He pointed at me and laughed some more. I was disbelieving, then disgusted. To have missed my shot and left the enemy alive and laughing— what a contradiction of my warrior ideal! In truth, I had not missed my shot. The arrow had grazed him, then veered and lodged in a pole. My stepfather had extraordinary spiritual powers, and it was not his fate to die by the arrow of a jealous child.

Nothing happened immediately because my mother was away, but when she came back and I ran up to greet her, she began to beat me. I doubt that Sodga himself told her about the incident, but others obviously had, and she was in a flaming temper. "Why, why, why did you do it?" she asked, shaking me and repeatedly striking me hard with her hand. In a way, I answered her. "I am your only son, and if you think this man is more important than I am, I will leave." I broke free of her and ran out the door.

It was late afternoon and I scrambled up the mountain

behind our house. I went on for a long time, gaining altitude rather than distance. Looking down, I could see our house on the bluff, the long valley below it and tiny yaks and horses drifting along up and down. Night was falling. I had decided that I would go to our herdsman's house and stay with him indefinitely. Then, in the still mountain air, I heard horses. Two men rode up the path. "Come with us, Tulku," one of them said. "Your mother sent us to bring you home, and it's almost dark." He dismounted and without protest I let him hoist me up into the saddle. He took the reins to lead my horse, and silently we all headed back. When I saw my mother she took me into her arms and embraced me, and we both wept. Nothing more was said about the shooting incident. Sodga decided to teach me the *Bodhicharyavatara,* Shantideva's classic text that elucidates all levels of proper conduct of the bodhisattva as the awakened warrior who uses each moment on the path of enlightenment as an opportunity to benefit others. I found his teaching wonderful.

MY STEPSISTER by Sodga was born in midwinter when I was ten. As Lama Tse Gon walked to my mother's house on the morning of her birth, he found a flower blooming in the snow. Everyone agreed this was an auspicious sign. As she grew up, it was clear that she was an unusual child. Some days she would wake up joyous, sing her mantra loudly and do energetic prostrations. Other days she would wake up sullen, stand in a corner muttering and throw a tantrum if anyone approached her.

Just as with me, my mother had received fair warning that an unusual child was on the way. In an area five days' ride from Tenp'hel Gonpa, a strange woman named Ugdrön lived under a bridge. She was very sleek and fat, though she had no food or outer support whatsoever. Her dog was also fat and healthy, though no one ever saw it eat. The inhabitants of the nearby village disliked and feared her, but they left her alone until a prolonged drought withered the area. In their desperation, the villagers decided the woman was a demoness and the source of their suffering. A mob gathered and trooped down to the bridge. They seized her, bound her up and threw her into the river to drown. To their amazement, she didn't sink but instead floated upstream.

An intense discussion ensued. Those who did not think it wise to leave her floating up the river finally prevailed. They fished her out and set her free; then they consulted several high lamas about her. The lamas said that she was not a demoness, but an emanation of the deity Dorje P'hagmo. The people left her alone after that and regarded her with respect. When pilgrims crossed her bridge, Ugdrön would hail them and ask their name and where they were from. They would answer and she would describe their family tree, for several generations back, including the realm of rebirth of the deceased. One day a group of people from Tenp'hel Gonpa went on a pilgrimage to a famous *stupa* a day's walk from Ugdrön's bridge. As they crossed the bridge, Ugdrön called to them, "Tell my mother, Delog Dawa Drolma, that I'm not staying here another year. I'm coming to visit her." When they returned to Tenp'hel Gonpa, the pilgrims gave this message to my mother. News followed that Ugdrön had died, and soon after my mother became pregnant and gave birth to my stepsister. She was named T'hrinlay Wangmo, "Mother of Powerful Activity."

LAMA TSE GON gave me a short, formal teaching each day and had me present the same teaching to him the following day to demonstrate my understanding. I continued to attend a number of the teachings he gave to the three-year retreat-ants. As the end of the retreat approached, he informed me that I would teach the preliminary practices—the foundation of all practices in Tibetan Vajrayana Buddhism—during the next three-year retreat. I took to heart the seriousness of this responsibility and began to probe more deeply the teachings I heard.

4

Retreat

THE MINISTER of the king of Dege requested that my mother come to his region to perform a ceremony. This invitation honored her renown as a lama and honored Tenp'hel Gonpa as the monastery with which she was associated. She was sent off with much fanfare.

Dege was the most important principality in Eastern Tibet and the hub of the central government. It was also the seat of Dege Gönchhen, a large monastery whose printery was one of the finest in all of Tibet. This printery produced an edition of the *Kanjur*, the Buddhist canon, that is still famous for the excellent quality of its wood blocks and the accuracy of its scholarship.

After the ceremony was completed, my mother addressed the minister's family: "As everything in this world is impermanent, who knows how long this body of mine will last? If I should die, I request that you of this noble family see that my two children are well cared for." The family agreed to do so.

When her words were repeated in Tenp'hel Gonpa, people became anxious that my mother's death was imminent, and there was a certain tentativeness in their interactions with her. I had just turned eleven, and she and Lama Tse Gon skillfully averted my own fears by focusing on my three-year retreat.

Lama Tse Gon had already indicated that I should give teachings on the preliminary practices to the retreatants, but now my mother said that I should join the retreat myself. Although the three-year retreat forms an integral part of a lama's training, I might not have begun one for another three years had my mother not told Lama Tse Gon that I should enter in a few months when the next group began.

In the eleventh month, the dead of winter, the retreat started. The night before it began, I had a horrifying dream. A naked and vicious woman brandishing a black cloth in her right hand chased me, and I knew I was in tremendous danger. I awoke very frightened and couldn't sleep for the rest of the night. Lama Tse Gon thought the woman in my dream was Galama, a local landholding spirit. Although the dream was not an auspicious sign, retreat started the next day nonetheless.

I spent the next three years of my life in the Tenp'hel Gonpa retreat building, which stood at the edge of the monastic community. There were no outside-facing windows in this structure, and the retreatants' small rooms faced an inner, open courtyard. It was a strict rule of retreat that one could neither look at nor be seen by anyone outside, and the building was designed with this in mind. The open shed that served as a latrine had a high wall around it. There were seven of us: Lama Tse Gon, Lama Atse, me, two other monks, the *gonla*—a practitioner who did continuous dharma protector practice to safeguard the path of practitioners— and an attendant. The attendant helped care for the shrine and made water offerings in one hundred and eight bowls every day. He brought us food and other supplies, and carried water on his back in and out of the retreat building.

Our days were structured through a series of formal meditation sessions. A gong silenced our chatter at the beginning of each session and reverberated through the meditative stillness at the end. The first session began very early, around three or four o'clock in the morning, and was followed by breakfast. Breakfast preparation had begun the preceding night. A clay pot with a thick lining of yak dung was filled with coals that burned slowly through the night. Above the pot hung a huge kettle filled with water and a handful of tea leaves, and this entire assembly was covered with a heavy fabric for insulation.

In the morning milk and butter were added to the steaming tea, and the buttered tea was mixed with *tsampa*—the roasted barley flour that is the staple of the Tibetan diet. We ate *tsampa* with dried cheese or yogurt three meals a day. If we were lucky, we had some dried meat to eat with it. Every day after breakfast we responded to the requests for prayers and offerings from local people, to alleviate the suffering of the sick, dying and recently deceased. The fire offering ceremony that we did on their behalf could extend well into the morning if there had been numerous appeals. For the remainder of the day, we did our main meditation practice, which varied as the retreat progressed. This was punctuated by short breaks for tea and lunch. After lunch, we often went up to the roof to clean sediment that had accumulated in the water bowls, polishing them until they gleamed in the midday sun.

At the end of the afternoon session, we said prayers for the benefit of the dead and did dharma protector practice. The accompaniment of drums, horns and trumpets inspired awe as sound filled the meditation hall and merged with the fading afternoon light. Dinner was brief, followed immediately by the day's last session, which we closed with *chod* practice.

Each night as I went to sleep in my meditation box, I implored Lama Tse Gon, whose box was next to mine, to tell me a story. He never refused, and told my favorite ones again and again. He knew a story about wild animals, a dog and an earthworm that was very poetic. He half chanted, half sang it to me, and I loved its cadence. He must have told it to me more than a hundred times, yet, sadly, it has completely slipped from my memory.

Although Lama Tse Gon was the main instructor for our retreat, a small throne was made for me in the shrine room, and I taught the preliminary practices I had heard Lama Tse Gon teach during the previous retreat. For the first four weeks, we did Wrathful Guru Rinpoche practice, a powerful method for cutting delusion at the root and removing obstacles arising from it. In our practice we focused particularly on clearing obstacles that might negate the benefit of our retreat.

Then we began the preliminary practices by contemplating four thoughts: the preciousness of our human birth, impermanence, karma and suffering. After this we performed strenuous body-length prostrations—one hundred thousand over a period of time—while visualizing the objects of spiritual refuge and reciting a refuge prayer. Prostrations are a physical expression of prayer which purify nonvirtue created through inappropriate use of one's body and honor the Buddha as the perfect teacher, the dharma as the perfect teaching and the sangha—the fellowship of Buddhist practitioners—as virtuous companions on the path. Sometimes I did my practice with sincere motivation and good heart, and maintained strong

visualization and recitation. At other times, I did it quickly
and by rote.

Lama Tse Gon was much larger than I, and he performed
his prostrations more slowly. So we each counted our own,
which offered me the opportunity to cheat, which I did
occasionally. In addition to sometimes miscounting my prostrations and mantra recitations, I peeked outside through a
small hole I found in the latrine wall, clearly a breach of the
rules. During the day, I could hear children playing outside
the retreat building, and my thoughts were instantly transported outdoors. I longed to romp with them and thought
how fortunate they were to play while I had to stay inside. I
felt deprived.

ABOUT FOUR MONTHS after I began retreat a messenger
arrived with news that altered my childhood completely. My
mother's death stunned me. She was young, still in her early
thirties, and I had not even known she was ill. When Lama
Tse Gon received the news, he immediately left retreat to
make preparations for the death ceremonies. I, too, left. I
needed to participate in all the ceremonies and to see my
mother one last time.

For three days after her death, her body was not touched.
Then it was washed with saffron water, wrapped in white
cloth and seated in the posture of White Tara. A crown and
the ornaments of the deity were placed on her head. For five
days more, hundreds of people came to pray and to pay their
last respects to one who had dedicated her life to others. She
had profoundly touched their lives—healing them and their
children, praying for their deceased relatives and helping them
resolve every kind of obstacle. Because she was a *delog,* some

people thought that she would return to life once again. Tonpa Tulku, however, replied, "She is not coming back now. She is in Guru Rinpoche's pureland and will remain there until another time."

My mother's body was cremated on the roof of her house. In each of the four directions sat a lama performing death practices. The body remained in meditation posture for many days and did not collapse in the cremation fire until it had nearly turned to ash. Rainbows spontaneously appeared in the clear blue sky. Five vultures circled the cremation fire and then flew away in unison. Four or five fingernail-sized relics were found in the ashes. These signs reflected the strength of my mother's practice and realization, proving that she had transcended death and ordinary rebirth.

As I watched the people mourning, the death ceremonies and the cremation fire, everything seemed hollow and empty. My mother's body, my own body, the world around me—all of it was infused with a fathomless sense of unreality. I had no thoughts. I never cried.

Lama Tse Gon spoke to me, "When your mother became ill, she told your stepfather and others who were present that I should give you this message. When she was pregnant with you, she had two dreams. In the first, a red man with a horse head came and merged with her stomach. In the second, a being with many heads was inside her, and each head was involved in a different activity. One played a conch, one sang, one taught and so forth, and each of these activities addressed a different, highly inspired audience.

"She said you should be told that these dreams were powerful signs that through your activity you can be of tremendous benefit to others. However, she also said that you must first dedicate yourself to the discipline of practice so that you can find release from an ordinary, self-centered perspective and recognize the absolute nature of mind. When you are able to abide in recognition of the absolute, you will be a source of immense benefit."

When the ceremonies were over, I returned to retreat. Soon after, my Uncle Tromge, my mother's brother, arrived at Tenp'hel Gonpa, having traveled for four or five days from Tromt'har. He had come to take my sister and me back with him.

My stepfather didn't think this was advisable, and they had a heated discussion about it. My stepfather wanted me to finish retreat. He also wanted to raise his own daughter. My uncle was adamant, insisting it was his responsibility to care for us now that our mother had died. Even then, as a child, I wondered if his motivation was not more complicated than that. My uncle liked wealth and could make good use of it to support his large household, and my mother had accumulated substantial wealth.

The issue of whether my sister and I would stay or go intensified when the monks and lamas of Tenp'hel Gonpa learned of my uncle's reason for being there. They did not want us to go and were vehement in their opposition. My stepfather, a wise and peaceable man, finally suggested that I was old enough to decide the issue myself.

A large delegation, including my stepfather and my uncle, came to the entrance of the retreat building. I was summoned from meditation to meet them. "Tulku," one of them said, "you are now eleven and your mother has died. Your uncle would like to take you with him. Your stepfather would like you to stay. What do you want to do?"

In replying, I made the first important speech of my life, and as I spoke, it was not from the experience of a child, but from a place of deep understanding. "I am not going," I said. "My mother brought me to this region, and she built the house where my stepfather and my young sister now live. It would not honor her for us to abandon this place. My mother foresaw her death and it was by her wish that I entered this retreat before she died. I would disrespect her wishes if I abandoned it."

I said that I was grateful to the representative of the minister of Dege—for true to his promise to my mother, the minister had offered to take in my stepfather, my stepsister and me—but told him that we did not need his assistance now.

"As far as my mother's wealth is concerned," I continued, "I don't need it. I believe I have the karma to have something to eat and something to wear. All of the offerings people have ever given for my mother's prayers and her help I now offer to the welfare of all beings.

"My mother's wish was to build a prayer wheel with ten million hundred-syllable Vajrasattva mantras in it. She asked her kind sponsor, Gerong Drilo, to complete it if she should die or otherwise be unable to carry it through."

I then addressed Drilo. "You, Drilo-la, I ask to take all my mother's wealth, including her herds of yak and sheep, convert it to cash and oversee the construction of the prayer wheel. When my mother's money has been totally spent for this purpose, please fulfill your own commitment to her and meet any additional expenses yourself."

To print ten million Vajrasattva mantras was very costly; the paper alone was almost thirteen thousand silver coins, a considerable fortune by anyone's standards. It was brought from China by yak, a journey of many months. The structure that housed the prayer wheel, as well as the wheel itself, was made of wood. We lived at such a high altitude that one had to travel for seven days to find wood—another big expense.

After my mother's death, the prayer wheel took two years to complete. It was an enormous, beautifully painted cylinder containing a huge roll of printed mantras. It was installed vertically in its own small building, and people could circumambulate it, rotating the cylinder by holding a handle as they walked. A bell at the top sounded at each revolution.

In the building that housed the prayer wheel, just large enough to allow circumambulation, the pulsation of the spinning mantras was like an actual experience of the pervasiveness of Vajrasattva's purification. This fulfilled my mother's intention that all persons who came there and prayed with faith would be cleansed of the obscuring habits and poisons of the mind, and that by the blessing of Vajrasattva's compassion and wisdom, all would come to abide in the intrinsic purity of their mind's absolute nature.

My mother's death powerfully reinforced for me how hopeless it is to grasp at what is impermanent. I had loved my mother and relied on her, as had my stepfather, my sister and many others, and her love and compassion for all of us were measureless. Yet these strong bonds had not prevented her from slipping from our grasp and dying. Even her wisdom realization, which transcended death, had not averted the loss of her body. Shortly before, my family had been very wealthy. Now that wealth had been freely given to the lamas who had conducted the death ceremonies and toward the completion of the prayer wheel. It was exactly as I had been taught. Wealth lasts no longer than the honey that bees gather.

As my attachments loosened, the dharma became richer and more meaningful to me. Lama Tse Gon's message about my mother's dreams spurred my wish to practice strongly and accomplish the realization I would need to benefit others in this life. My mother's cremation was equally inspiring to me. I wanted the spiritual power to die as flawlessly as she had.

AFTER SIX MONTHS in retreat, we had completed the preliminary practices except for guru yoga—the pivotal meditation practice that melds one's own heart essence with the heart essence of all those who have previously attained realization of absolute wisdom, especially one's own lama. This took three months more. During that time, we meditated in our own small rooms, until the last seven days, when we gathered in the shrine room and practiced together.

My retreat had gotten off to an uncertain start in the first months, as I cheated on my prostrations and mantra recitations, but when I returned to retreat after my mother's death my practice became much more purposeful.

We followed the preliminaries with the deity practices of Chakrasamvara and Vajra Yogini. At times my mind was very tight and angry, but after a while these emotions subsided and I had good signs in my dreams and visions. Several times I had dreams of goddesses surrounding me, presenting offerings. Upon completing these practices, I had a dream that people were gathering for a feast. Song filled the air, and I partook of the vast quantities and varieties of food that were being served.

AT ONE POINT early in retreat, we were requested to take care of a scholar named Khanpo Tanrab who had become very ill. He was only about fifty years old, but the uncle who had been his attendant was too old to look after him properly. He needed very intensive care, being unable to turn over or to get to the latrine. We placed his bed in a central location where everyone could tend to him. When *puja* was finished, we went to his bed to make certain that he was all right. He was very kind and loving toward me and I liked to be around him. When I went near him, he held my hand or touched my arm with great tenderness.

One night as I slept, I saw my room, the monastery and the surrounding landscape very clearly, as if I were awake. I watched a very powerful man approach the monastery. Leopard skin lined the edges of his robes, on his head was a tiger skin hat and in his hand he carried a potent wandlike implement with a silver handle. He came straight to the retreat house door. When he became aware that I saw him, he motioned to me to be quiet. He touched my face, from my mouth to my right cheek, with the wand. Then he went to Khanpo Tanrab. Though I couldn't tell what he was doing, I saw him leave carrying a basket on his back filled with chunks of meaty flesh.

When I awoke the next day, there was a swelling on my face as thick as my finger where he had touched me. Lama Tse Gon saw it and, upon learning what had happened, became very concerned. He sent a message to Chagmo Tulku, the abbot of the monastery, to come because there was an obstacle to our retreat. When I recounted my experience to the abbot, he told me that the man I had seen was a wealthholding demon and that this incident was extremely unfortunate. Lama Tse Gon was worried about Khanpo Tanrab. He and the other retreatants decided that the next morning they would perform a *dur,* a practice for removing obstacles.

The *khanpo* seemed fine and he called me over to his bedside. Now, however, I felt uncomfortable going near him. Such a strong distaste arose in me that I went to great pains to avoid any contact with him. As soon as the *dur* began the next morning, the *khanpo*'s condition deteriorated. Movement became so difficult for him that he was barely able to lift the fingers of his right hand as it lay on his chest. His breath became more labored and death rattled in his throat. He died in the early afternoon, before the *dur* ceremony had been completed.

Immediately, the weather changed. Huge gusts of wind kicked up dust and spun violently throughout the valley. The density of the dust storm lent the appearance of dusk to the afternoon landscape. Lama Tse Gon called for Tonpa Tulku, the very elderly lama for whom my mother had done the long-life ceremony blessed by the miraculous multiplication of pills. Upon the *tulku*'s arrival, rather than doing the requested death practice, he immediately began to sing in fractured, aged tones the pure vision *chod* practice of Dudjom Lingpa, to cut through obstacles.

As he finished the last verse, there was a knock at the door and in walked the nephew of Tulku Gyurmed Namchag Dorje, the very old and bedridden lama whose life had been extended by my mother's move to Tenp'hel Gonpa. Stirring briefly from his sleep, the old lama had told his nephew, "Now Khanpo has died. His body must not remain in the retreat house overnight. A fast horse and rider must immediately be sent to the Futsu region to bring the *chodpa* Asam." Then he fell back asleep.

As soon as the nephew brought the message, Lama Tse Gon sent out a rider. Anxiety was escalating, and we did the death practice so quickly that it may not have been effective.

We placed the body in a storage shed behind the building and waited for the *chodpa*. We feared that if he did not arrive that night, a demonic entity would possess the *khanpo*'s body, reanimating it as a zombie.

The *chodpa* finally arrived late in the evening and had us make him a bed in the storage shack near the corpse, which was now swelling and exuding blood. There he spent the night. The next morning, blood from the corpse was splattered throughout the shed and the *khanpo*'s body had resumed its normal proportions. He was given a sky burial, the flesh removed from the bones and fed to the vultures as a final offering.

Many people felt that the *khanpo*'s arrogance had created this horrific death. He was a very fine scholar who upheld his monk's vows perfectly. But he was also self-righteous and frequently found fault with those around him. This experience was deeply imprinted in my mind. As I realized the extent to which pride hurts not only oneself, but others as well, I vowed to remain vigilant, lest it develop in me as well.

AT THIS POINT in retreat, we began to learn the six yogas of Naropa. This practice involves many kinds of yogic postures and rather athletic meditations. I was good at these, perhaps because I was young and agile, and I found them to be extremely beneficial. Lama Tse Gon was a wonderful yoga teacher, very limber and energetic. We were introduced to a number of practices of the winds and channels, including generating inner heat (*tummo*), dream yoga, recognition of illusion and mastering the inner energy essences (*t'higlé*).

Lama Atse wanted to do all the yogas but Lama Tse Gon tried to discourage him, thinking that at his age it might be extremely difficult. Lama Atse would hear none of it. "I must! I must!" he insisted. "I don't want to let this great fortune and opportunity pass me by. I will do whatever needs to be done." So Lama Tse Gon taught us how to do *beps,* controlled falls that clear the body's subtle channels. The very first time that Lama Atse tried to do one, he fell back on his tail. For the next six days, he could barely sit, much less do any yoga.

Although he was not accomplished at the yogas, Lama Atse brought extraordinary qualities to my retreat. He was a *siddha,* meaning that he had direct realization of absolute truth. Almost daily, Lama Atse stopped somewhere in the *puja* to explain its inner meaning to me, and a vast understanding began to unfold. During this period, he had numerous dreams in which he saw me doing *chod* practice in the company of many strange-looking people, with faces and bodies unlike any he had ever seen. I took note and remembered his dreams years later as I practiced *chod* throughout India, Nepal and the United States.

Every evening, I made offerings to the dharma protectors, particularly to Gesar, Tibet's epic hero, and Tagtzan, Tenp'hel Gonpa's main protector. I used a tiny ceramic offering cup called a *serkyem* that Lama Tse Gon's brother had brought me from China. One night as I lay in a mental twilight between waking and sleep, the whole valley appeared before my eyes. An enormous white cloud billowed in the sky above a horse that approached from the right side of the valley with huge, thundering strides. On his back rode a beautiful man wearing white robes and a white hat with a peacock feather in the top. A bow and arrow hung from his right side, a bow and sword from his left, and through the crook of his arm he carried a spear covered with banners that flapped in the wind. He held his left hand in a symbolic gesture and in his right hand he held a whip. I recognized him as the protector Tagtzan.

From the left side of the valley, a whirling black-red vortex of fire and wind surrounded a red horse and rider wearing armor with a breastplate and a helmet with different colored flags, the central flag a victory banner, symbolizing the awakened mind. I knew that this rider was Gesar. Both riders were as massive as mountains. As they approached, I spread my arms toward them with my palms facing upward, and they alighted in the center of each hand. Then I awoke.

DURING THE LATTER HALF of my retreat, I was in a state of *nyam,* extraordinary visionary experience. Though *nyam* does not represent stable realization, it may reflect a relaxation of one's ordinary perception of reality. For several months, I could see as if there were no walls in my room and I could read in the dark after the butterlamps were out. I could also see beings living in other realms of existence.

At one point during a meditation session, I watched thousands of people gathering in tents in the large field across the river from the monastery grounds. Three men left the community, crossed the river and the grounds, entered the main building of the monastery and strode into the room of the *umzé,* or chanter. This *umzé* was an exceptional chanter and his resonant voice had a marvelous capacity for projection. The men emerged from his room carrying something away.

Lama Tse Gon was very disturbed when I told him what I had seen. He sent for Chagmo Tulku, and they decided a *puja* must be done immediately. The *umzé* felt very ill the next day as they began the *puja,* and by late afternoon he had a high fever. In the early evening, he died. Although the *puja* may have appeared ineffective, we felt fortunate that no one else died, since my vision had indicated the possibility of a massive epidemic. I had visions such as these quite often, and Lama Tse Gon and Lama Atse had great respect for the insights the visions revealed: they were usually very accurate.

There was a lama named Wangkhyug Tulku who lived in the monastery at Tenp'hel Gonpa while I was on retreat. He was about eighteen years old, a monk, but one who enjoyed the company of women and who created merriment and laughter wherever he went. One day, however, he got into a ferocious argument with another monk and stormed to the *gonla*'s room, which was filled with implements of the dharma protector practice. Seizing a sword, with a sudden motion he knotted the heavy iron blade into the letter *cha*. Overcome with envy, I secretly went over to our own retreat shrine and pulled a sword out from under it. Straining every muscle, I tried to bend the blade. It didn't give at all. I humbly crept away.

The end of retreat was drawing near, and I began to contemplate the life that awaited me on the other side of the retreat house wall. I knew that the monastic system provided a strong foundation for pure practice, yet more often than not, the strong practitioners among monks and nuns would decide that it was time to leave the monastery. They wanted to enter a solitary retreat or to study intensively with one lama. Although I lived completely within the monastic order, I was inspired by the style and stories of great yogis, such as Milarepa and Naropa, who cut through delusions, escaped the entrapping web of attachment and aversion, hope and fear and attained profound realization of their mind's true nature.

One day, as I sat in the shrine room facing the statues of Milarepa, Marpa and Gampopa, I contemplated my dilemma and prayed before these great yogis. As I did, the statue of Milarepa seemed to come alive, to look at me and smile. A great tension was suddenly released, and I wept for a long time, resolving right then to follow the path of the yogi in this life.

Soon after, the time came for me and one other retreatant to demonstrate the power of our inner heat (*tummo*) practice. A *tulku* from Tenp'hel Gonpa, the elder retreatants and several other yogis were summoned to examine us. To pass the test we would have to wrap a series of wet sheets around our naked bodies and dry the sheets by the inner heat we generated through yogic exercises and meditation. It was the middle of winter and extremely cold. I was afraid that my teeth would chatter, my sheets would not dry and I would be ridiculed.

The monk and I took our seats and opened the session with prayer. Then we began the yoga exercises and I thought, "Why be afraid? I have trained well and at my age that is auspicious in itself." Suddenly confidence flooded me and I easily dried one freezing sheet, then another. We stood up, circled the monastery and, as we came back to the front, the little gathering of people honored us by offering us white ceremonial scarves.

The next day, my three-year retreat ended. I was fourteen years old.

JUST BEFORE the conclusion of the retreat, Lama Tse Gon gave wool cloth, bolts of silk and lambskins to a tailor and had him sew for me new robes and a *zen,* the long cloth that is wrapped over one's upper robes as the vestment of a monk or lama. He also had a fine hat made, with fox fur on the front flap. On the day of my exit, a horse was groomed to perfection and decked out with a colorful saddle carpet and various ornaments. I enjoyed the handsome display of it all as I left the confines of the retreat compound, mounted my horse and rode in procession through the admiring crowds. For about six months I traveled with the other retreatants, performing ceremonies at the request of various families in the area. I was in the full flush of my retreat accomplishments and didn't hesitate to demonstrate them. For example, if it suddenly began to rain or snow, I would blow into the air and the rain or snow would stop by the power of my accumulations of mantra. At the age of fourteen such minor feats might have seduced me into catastrophic pride except for the intervention of failure.

I had been invited to do prayers and ceremonies for a woman who had died in a place fifteen miles away. The weather in the mountains of Eastern Tibet is extremely changeable, and my attendant sensibly suggested we take the felt cloaks we used as raincoats.

"There's no need," I replied. "If it rains I can stop it easily." We rode off, and on the way not a drop fell. On the way back, however, it poured, a cold, drenching, relentless rain that didn't give way one moment to the puffing of my breath. My attendant, again sensibly, said nothing. I did not glance his way.

I lived in the home of my stepfather and stepsister during this period, although most often I was away taking teachings from other lamas. Tibet was dwelling in the twilight of the great epoch of Buddhism that had begun in the nineteenth century. As if blessed by the brilliance of many suns, the land abounded in splendidly accomplished lamas. During this time of relative peace both scholarship and practice were flourishing and sectarianism waning. Soon the Chinese vise would tighten, but at that time it was still fairly easy for me to receive empowerments and instruction from Jamyang Khyentse Chhökyi Lodrö, Sechhen Kongtrul, Khanpo Bat'hur, Khanpo Ngaga and others. With a joyous sense of high purpose, I explored the meaning and methods of the Buddha's teaching. Free from the forced discipline of my childhood and the three-year retreat, I studied diligently, wanting to know everything. I was absorbed by the discourses of my lamas, inspired by their examples. The fiery currents of energy that created so much conflict in my earlier years were now more manageable within my mind, though occasionally their unabated presence would be evidenced by a volcanic eruption.

MY PURPOSE in making a four-day journey to Dzongsar Monastery to meet Jamyang Khyentse Chhökyi Lodrö was primarily to request that he locate three *tulkus* associated with Tenp'hel Gonpa. Jamyang Khyentse was an authority on all traditions in Tibet and served as the heart of the ecumenical (*rimé*) movement in Eastern Tibet. He honored my request to locate the *tulkus* using an extraordinary process that only very great lamas can accomplish reliably. Through the appearances that arose in his meditation, he was able to see the physical and personality traits of each of the *tulkus* and give precise details as to how to find them. Discerning this information took some time, however, and while I waited at his monastery I had the great fortune to participate in a series of empowerments he was giving into the Rinchhen Terdzod, a large collection of texts hidden by Padmasambhava as *termas* and revealed by various lamas. These empowerments later became part of the very foundation of my practice. During the empowerments my attention was drawn to an uncommonly tall lama with very long hair who sat next to Khyentse Chhökyi Lodrö and sometimes participated in the preparations. Inquiring about him, I learned that his name was Dilgo Khyentse and he was known for his extraordinary qualities as a treasure discoverer. I went up to receive his blessing and felt a deep current of faith stir as his hand touched my head. In the future he would become one of my most revered teachers.

Later, after I returned to Tenp'hel Gonpa, the three *tulkus* were located exactly as Khyentse Chhökyi Lodrö had foretold, and their enthronements became major events. It was my responsibility to give the ceremonial oration for each one—a daunting task for a fourteen-year-old because Tibet is a country of orators and my speech was expected to match the illustrious occasion. Still, those who heard me seemed to approve and I was asked to speak the next year, and the next.

WHEN I WAS SIXTEEN, my uncle came from Tromt'har to request that I join a ceremony to invoke the dharma protectors of the Sakya lineage of Tibetan Buddhism. It was almost Losar, Tibetan New Year, and an auspicious time for a reunion with my maternal relatives.

Some fifty monks were doing protector practice when I arrived and took my place. During the tea break, one fat monk, about sixty years old and quite formidable looking, started to question me.

"What is the tradition of the monastery where you've been living?"

"Drukpa Kagyu."

"Too bad! Those Karma Kagyus, Drukpa Kagyus and Bonpos are really just thieves of the Buddha's doctrine."

This was a startling insult to the lineage lamas I revered and to me as a lineage holder. If he had said, "Your father is a scoundrel and you are a bastard," he could not have been more provocative. I collected myself before I replied.

"You think what you think, of course, but for me the dharma is like a ball of sugar, sweet wherever you taste it. Like milk, it tastes the same no matter where you stand to drink it. Like gold, it is gold no matter how you slice through it. The Sakya, the Gelug, the Kagyu and the Nyingma are all dharma, essentially the same."

The practice resumed and I would have been happy to let the matter drop at that point, but the next day during lunch the monk confronted me again.

"Do you accept the fact that phenomena are your own mind, none other than your own mind?"

From his tone I took this as a challenge to debate, which in the Tibetan tradition is a stylized intellectual contest to prove one's own point, or at least destroy the other person's premise. Debate is the sport of Buddhist scholars and is extremely competitive. At my age, I had no great confidence in myself as a scholar, but I could not ignore the monk's challenge without disgracing myself and my teachers, so I made a forceful reply. "No, it is not that phenomena are only one's own mind. And yet without the mind, how would there be any experience of phenomena? It is like the ocean and a wave. If someone pointed to a wave and said, 'What is that?' you

65

would say, 'That is a wave.' And yet a wave is nothing other than the ocean.

"Similarly, it cannot be said that phenomenal reality is only one's own mind, but both the day experience and the dream experience are based in one's mind. Yet by day the dream experience disappears and the mind remains; by night the waking experience disappears and the mind remains."

I had answered the monk according to my understanding and my actual experience of the nature of phenomena, but in the combative tone of debate. To my surprise he made no reply. Then I realized that he was neither a scholar nor prepared to debate. So I let the matter drop.

One day a delegation of fifteen Chagdud Gonpa monks rode up to my family's tent. We extended hospitality to them, but they quickly got to the point. They wanted me to make the two-day journey to my monastery. "We have made this request many times before," the leader of the delegation said, "but again and again your mother delayed your visit, the last time by saying that you must do your retreat first. Now that your retreat is complete, we request that you come straightaway." Without hesitation, I agreed and shortly after rode off with them to Nyagrong, the region where Chagdud Gonpa is located. As in a dream that recurs with some elements constant and some changed, I was returning once more to the place that had been pivotal to my spiritual activities for fifteen past lifetimes.

5

Chagdud Gonpa

WE TRAVELED to Chagdud Gonpa through the long, narrow valley of the Nyagchu River. Nyagrong is a region of steep, ten-thousand-foot mountains covered with dense evergreen forests. In a time beyond the reckoning of time, Nyagrong received the blessing of Manjushri, Avalokiteshvara and Vajrapani. During the reign of the great dharma king Srongtzan Gampo in the seventh century, one hundred and eight *stupas* were miraculously manifested by *yakshas* and horse lords, supernatural beings from realms unseen by humans.

In the eighth century Padmasambhava, his consort Yeshe Tsogyal and the great translator Vairocana visited these *stupas*, representations of the nature of mind that also served as border markers for King Srongtzan Gampo's empire. Padmasambhava found the region to be a good place for the practice of dharma, outwardly secured by the dharma protectors, inwardly blessed by the presence of the lord of compassion Avalokiteshvara and secretly a realm of his own pureland of Padma Od (Lotus Light). During their sojourn in the region, these three consecrated many sacred sites and concealed many *termas* to benefit future practitioners.

In 1214 Dritsa Gangpa, one of the four dharma heirs of the preeminent Nyingma lama Kat'hog Dampa Desheg, built the first monastery on the site that would become Chagdud Gonpa. Though he had built more than one hundred monasteries, he extolled this one as having been established under the most auspicious circumstances. It flourished as a center of the *sutra* and *tantra* teachings, but eventually it was overthrown and reduced to ruins by the partisans of a rival monastery. The area then reverted to the ancient shamanistic tradition of Bon, and the incarnations of Dritsa Gangpa took their rebirths in India, Nepal and elsewhere.

In Tibet, meanwhile, one named Nyag Jnanakumara—an emanation of the enlightened mind of Padmasambhava—took rebirth as the lama of Yeshe Gyaltsan and is said to have "caused the teachings of the victorious ones to shine like the sun" during his lifetime. One evening, as he approached the end of his life, a pure vision arose of *dakinis* escorting him along a path of silken ribbons, prophesying the place and circumstances of his next rebirth, and his name. Accordingly, Sherab Gyaltsan—the first in the line of Chagduds and the one who would cause Chagdud Gonpa to rise from the ashes of destruction—was born in 1398.

At the age of twenty-five, Sherab Gyaltsan recalled his former existence as Nyag Jnanakumara and went to Kat'hog Gonpa, where he received monastic ordination, bodhisattva vows and Vajrayana vows and quickly mastered all levels of teaching and meditation. Then Padmasambhava, mounted on a lion in the sky, appeared to him and said, "Son, go back to your home country and benefit beings by founding a monastery there." In 1431 he built a monastery on the site of the ruins of Dritsa Gangpa's monastery and named it Orgyan Khadro Bumling, "Place of the Hundred Thousand Dakinis of Orgyan."

Some years later Sherab Gyaltsan served the Mongol emperor of China as spiritual adviser. He demonstrated his erudition and many extraordinary signs of his spiritual attainment. In particular, he turned the barrel of the emperor's gun inside out, tied nine knots in it and made an offering of it to create auspicious conditions free of war and social unrest. It is because of this power to tie iron into knots that Sherab Gyaltsan came to be known as Chagdud (Iron Knot). The emperor in turn bestowed upon him a high rank in a testimony written on a scroll in gold ink. The emperor also placed the entire Nyag Valley under the administration of Chagdud Orgyan Khadro Bumling, and at the zenith of its power all the valley's monastic communities would assemble during the summer and winter solstices, a gathering of more than four thousand monks. Chagdud Sherab Gyaltsan established some twenty-five branch monasteries for his students, and more than two hundred practitioners were in full retreat at any given time.

In the five centuries after Chagdud Sherab Gyaltsan, Chagdud Gonpa continued to be held, through many vicissitudes of fortune, by a succession of Chagdud *tulkus*. My previous incarnation, Chagdud Tanpai Gyaltsan, had a short but remarkable life. Tanpai Gyaltsan lived with his teacher, Nyagla Yeshe Dorje, who was remarkable as well. Nyagla had been an expert and enthusiastic hunter until one day, as he rested on a rock, a vision of an eleven-headed

Avalokiteshvara appeared before him. Overwhelmed by this manifestation of pure compassion, he came to a profound understanding of how wrong it is to hunt and kill. He put aside his gun and instead of game sought out the Buddha's teachings. After he had listened well, he practiced ceaselessly, day and night. Since he would not take time to collect firewood himself, a huge, *yeti*-like creature with hair all over his body brought him wood. Eventually Nyagla Yeshe Dorje attained rainbow body—at the time of his death, the elements of his body, except for his hair and nails, instantly dissolved into a spectrum of light.

One day a man from a distant region approached Nyagla's home. The traveler carried a silk-wrapped scroll with a symbolic image of someone who had recently died. Through prayers and meditation, the consciousness of the dead person had been stabilized in the Sanskrit seed syllable in the image, and the traveler planned to ask Nyagla to transfer the consciousness into a state of liberation.

A little boy was playing on the road to the house and, seeing the traveler, asked what was in the pretty silk cloth. When the traveler explained, the boy begged him to let him see it. The traveler refused at first, but the child pleaded so intensely that at last he unrolled the scroll. The little boy gazed at it with deep concentration for a while, then thanked the traveler and went back to his play.

Upon meeting Nyagla, the traveler offered him a valuable piece of turquoise and another of coral. The lama opened the scroll and turned to the man in surprise. "What happened on your way here?" he asked.

"Nothing unusual," replied the traveler.

"You didn't show this scroll to anyone?"

"Only to the little boy on the road outside your house."

Nyagla looked out the window at the child. Handing the offerings back to the traveler, he said, "The consciousness of this person has already been transferred by the boy. You may give these offerings to him. His name is Chagdud Tanpai Gyaltsan."

Chagdud Tanpai Gyaltsan had the same masterful perspective on reality as Chagdud Sherab Gyaltsan. As *siddhas* they could completely comprehend in the same instant both the details of the phenomenal appearances that arose and the empty, dreamlike nature of these appearances. Not attributing any inherent existence, permanence or solidity to appearances, they were able to manipulate them spontaneously. For example, one day Chagdud Tanpai Gyaltsan, who had been drinking a good quantity of *arak,* rode up to a friend's house. There was no place to tie his horse so he stabbed his riding crop into a rock to make a post. It was a completely unrehearsed gesture, an action beyond concept. In a way it was of no particular benefit—there are other ways to secure horses—yet the demonstration of the nonsolid nature of that rock certainly benefited those who witnessed it and those who had faith in the truth of the tale.

Chagdud Tanpai Gyaltsan demonstrated extraordinary qualities of spiritual attainment again and again, yet he was not beyond karmic circumstances. Even though he knew he would die unless he made a journey to the sacred place of Tzari, he could not overcome obstacles to the pilgrimage. So he died at a young age, twenty-eight, not long after he had met my mother Dawa Drolma and offered her the reliquary that foretold his rebirth as her son.

SOME OF THE HISTORY of Chagdud Gonpa and the Chagdud incarnations I had heard before, some I learned from the

71

monks who escorted me through Nyagrong, some were spontaneously revealed within my mind.

At last we turned from the trail along the river and began the steep ascent of several thousand feet up to the monastery. The upper ridges of the mountain were cultivated with barley and dotted with small settlements. As we approached the highest ridge, the site of Chagdud Gonpa, we were greeted by throngs of people who formed a corridor almost a mile long.

The great carved doors of the monastery had been thrown open and I was escorted to the high throne. One by one people came up to offer me *katags* and receive my blessing. They also offered me bottles of *arak,* since that was what they were in the habit of offering Chagdud Tanpai Gyaltsan, and I sipped it steadily as it was served to me in a wooden cup that had been owned by him.

After some time, I announced to the assembly, "Now I will do a divination." I picked up a Tibetan text, which like all Tibetan texts was a compilation of loose pages between two boards. "I will throw this text out a window. If the pages scatter, it will indicate that my teachings will flourish in this place; if not, my teachings will take root elsewhere." Everyone was confident of the outcome, because strong winds whip incessantly across the high ridge on which Chagdud Gonpa is situated, yet when I tossed the book from a high window, not even one page took flight. All who witnessed this were dismayed.

After the ceremonies in the monastery, I received people in a private room. A man walked in unannounced, and as soon as I saw him, I said fiercely, "Dzug Tsering, why have you come here? You had no faith in me in my last life and you have no faith in me now. And since I have no need to pass some test of yours, you can leave." Suddenly I seized a charcoal brazier and for a moment it seemed as if I would fling it at him. Instead, with a jerk of the brazier, I spilled out the burning coals over my own head. As coals tumbled down my robes, everyone leapt up to gather them and were amazed that there were no burns or scorch marks.

Drug Tsering began making reverent prostrations before me. He had been the brother-in-law of Chagdud Tanpai Gyaltsan and had harbored animosity toward the lama. Even as he approached my room to greet me, he had boasted, "If this is really the *tulku* of Tanpai Gyaltsan, he will know me. If he doesn't know me, he is only a fraud." His wife and the others admonished him not to be so disrespectful, but he was very arrogant. After our encounter everyone agreed that all auspicious signs were present and there was no doubt of my being the incarnation of Chagdud Tanpai Gyaltsan.

Many years later I told this story to Tromge Trungpa Rinpoche. "You know," he commented, "you must measure the degree of realization not so much in your feat with the coals as in your recognition of your mind's awareness as it all happened." By this he was helping me to discriminate between ordinary *siddhis,* such as psychic powers and miraculous displays, and the extraordinary *siddhi* of attaining unwavering recognition of mind's true nature.

I stayed at Chagdud Gonpa for one week, then traveled to various homes in Nyagrong conducting ceremonies, talking with people and drinking *arak,* for which I had quite a taste. One evening, while I was drinking and enjoying the jovial atmosphere, a man named Kazang Dorje brought me a short, stout iron sword. Effortlessly, I folded it into four ripples. Those who witnessed it were awestruck, and also pleased that I had lived up to the name of Chagdud.

FINALLY, after so much going about, it was time to resume my formal training. My stepfather and Lama Tse Gon took me to Bat'hur Khanpo T'hubga, a superb and very unusual teacher. He was about sixty-five years old and had had no aspiration to build a monastery. He stayed in a large tent that could house a hundred monks. For the numerous wanderers who stopped at his camp to receive teachings, he created an ingenious method of housing. Each visitor dug up squares of sod and stacked them to form the walls of a tiny house, a cubicle whose inner dimensions corresponded to the length of its resident's body. The *khanpo* supplied a piece of black felt as the roof.

The *khanpo* was sometimes offered a *dri,* a female yak, and he had the milk, yogurt and butter it produced distributed to the practitioners in their little sod huts. The dung from the lama's animals was used by the practitioners as fuel.

I came with my own tent and stayed for a year and a half along with Lama Tse Gon. During this time I studied the texts of the great Indian Buddhist saints Shantideva and Nagarjuna. I received a thorough grounding in the philosophical tenets of the Madhyamika. The *khanpo* would teach first, giving an uninterrupted discourse on the doctrine. Another lama would follow, reviewing what the *khanpo* had said and answering our questions. None of us took notes until these classes were over. Then we would go to our tents and write down whatever we could remember of the day's teaching. The rest of the day was for study.

I made a point of reading my notes again and again, sometimes as many as thirty or forty times. My motivation for such study was mixed. We were learning the classics of Mahayana Buddhism and I wanted to be versed in them, and I respected the *khanpo* too much to take this opportunity lightly. However, another incentive to study was P'hurtse, who was a year older, jealous and competitive and who wished to outrival me as a scholar. I could not ignore his challenge.

Consistency was his strength and chance sometimes favored him. Each day a name was drawn to determine who would offer a rendition of the previous day's discourse in front of the *khanpo,* the second lama and the assembly of lamas and monks who were students. Whenever I guessed that I wouldn't be called, inevitably my name was drawn. My discomfort was compounded by P'hurtse's satisfaction. After several such occasions, I became quite consistent myself and accomplished my studies well.

SOON AFTER my return to Tenp'hel Gonpa I left again, this time for Sechhen Gonpa, an easy half-day's ride away. There I studied with Sechhen Kongtrul for eight months. I had received my first formal teachings on the nature of mind from him when I was eight years old. Though not extensive, these teachings were very precious. Now he agreed to instruct me privately in Mahamudra, the mind teachings known as the "Great Seal." This was an immense privilege, because he rarely saw anyone and normally remained in semiretreat. When this instruction was completed, he elucidated a number of classic Buddhist texts by Nagarjuna for me and another *tulku.*

Sechhen Kongtrul dedicated his life completely to the Buddha's teachings. If someone spoke to him about ordinary matters, the burden of listening would show on his face. If someone spoke of dharma, his delight was equally transparent. I felt deeper devotion for him as my teacher than I had ever experienced before. I applied myself to Mahamudra practice daily, and I felt his profound blessing in my meditation.

Sometime after I had left Sechhen Gonpa, I was returning to Tenp'hel Gonpa after performing death ceremonies at a village that was three days' ride away. A long caravan appeared in the distance, obviously an important lama and his retinue.

"Tulku, I wonder who that lama is? Should we ride down and meet him?" my attendant asked.

"No," I answered. "If we meet the lama, we will have to dismount and remount our horses. It will be easier to go a different way and avoid the caravan." It is difficult to get on or off a horse in Tibet because often the cinch gives way, the saddle twists and the rider tumbles to the ground.

We changed direction and rode along a high ridge to stay clear of the caravan. Then we cut down the mountainside to cross a river. On the opposite side of the river, we rode up over a steep embankment. To our amazement there was Sechhen Kongtrul resting with his attendant. It had been his caravan we had seen in the distance. While he rested, the other members of his retinue had gone on ahead.

The monk and I leapt off our horses and did prostrations. Sechhen Kongtrul placed his hands on my head and blessed me, saying, "Meditate more strongly."

That was all he said, then he rode on. As I stood there, filled with the power of his blessing, things seemed different, as if my perspective on reality had shifted. I was completely calm, devoid of any agitation in my mind.

The next day this calm remained, yet it had subtly changed. The initial pure, spontaneous experience of blessing had become stained with attachment and rigidified into a static state I wished to sustain. I went on a picnic with all the monks from Tenp'hel Gonpa. I felt distanced from the others as I watched them dash about, joking and playing. Later we performed a ceremony and I felt more distant still.

"No one is really meditating," I thought. "It's quite sad. The people place so much hope and faith in the lamas and monks. But they are only mindlessly chanting the words, and nothing will come of such practice."

Solemnly, I left the group to meditate. My mind became very settled; there seemed no reason not to sit there forever. Few thoughts arose, and I was comfortable. After a while my attendant came up with my horse, saying, "Tulku, it's time to leave."

Getting up slowly, I mounted my horse. When we reached the monastery, he helped me down and placed a saddle blanket and carpet on the ground so I could sit while he took care of the horse. Again I settled into a deep, stable, meditative calm. Sights and sounds seemed far away. Nothing firmly engaged my senses or my intellect. I experienced only fathomless tranquillity.

After a while, my attendant approached me and said, "Tulku, let's go to your house." Slowly, ponderously, I allowed myself to be led to the house, where I sat down on my bed and resumed my meditation. By this time my attendant was quite alarmed and urgently tried to communicate with me. But I didn't feel like responding. His conversation seemed vacuous.

He took leave of me and went to the room of one very poor lama. Some people thought this lama was a dubious character, but when my attendant went to him saying, "I need your advice. Tulku seems very strange . . ." the lama hit the mark.

"Oh, that's nothing," he scoffed. "He has just gotten himself lost in some state of meditative stability. Go shake him up and as he starts to come out of it say something insulting."

My attendant did just that—he shook me roughly. Like someone roused from sleep, I protested, "What do you think you're doing?" Then he said something very insulting that made me furious. Simultaneously, I felt as though a big, black hat had been lifted from my head.

My attendant apologized immediately, and as he explained the lama walked in.

"What are you doing?" he asked.

"Nothing now," I replied, "but what happened?"

He explained that I had been meditating with attachment to conceptless stability, and this attachment had resulted in heavy, flawed meditation.

So I had been powerfully blessed twice in two days, once by the revered Sechhen Kongtrul, once by that ragged, disreputable lama who cut short my wrong turn of mind.

FROM KHANPO JAMPAL ZANGPO I received an empowerment into the hundred peaceful and wrathful deities and teachings on the six *bardos*. He also empowered me into *chod,* and I went to many dangerous places to accomplish the practice. As had been foretold long ago in my vision of P'hadampa Sangye, father of the *chod* lineage, I had many miraculous experiences as a *chodpa*. Khanpo Jampal Zangpo told me not to speak of them at all.

OF ALL MY ILLUSTRIOUS TEACHERS during this period, perhaps none was more pivotal to my development than my stepfather Sodga. He was unfailingly patient and wise in his guardianship, and though he usually deferred to other lamas in my training, he ensured that the sequence was correct and complete. Above all, it was he I turned to as I struggled with that thorniest of issues for any young lama, the decision whether to remain celibate and therefore whether to remain a monk.

My stepfather was born and trained in the Gelugpa tradition and was affiliated with Bumsar Gonpa, a monastery three days' ride from Tenp'hel Gonpa. Near the monastery was a very sacred and powerful cave. Practitioners had come there for generations, until, for reasons no one understood, several meditators at different times became despondent while practicing there and hanged themselves. Suicide was an almost unheard of occurrence in Tibet before the Chinese takeover and contradicts the teachings of the Buddha. Practitioners and lay people alike began to avoid the cave as a repository of unspeakable horror.

To the dismay of his *gegan,* my stepfather, at the age of twelve, began demanding that he practice in this cave. The *gegan* refused, at first by trying to reason with the boy, then by asserting his authority. My stepfather became more insistent. It turned into a battle of wills, and Sodga prevailed.

When they reached the cave, Sodga entered alone and settled into his practice immediately. Without Sodga's consent, the *gegan* remained outside the cave and did his own practice. Now and then he peeked protectively at the boy in the cave. Nothing seemed amiss. The boy continued to practice, and when night fell, he seemed to sleep. His fears allayed, the *gegan* went back to the monastery.

Very early the next morning the *gegan* returned to the cave and looked in on the boy. He was still there meditating, but the night had been eventful. In the cave he had found a large stone disk formed of two disks sealed together. Centuries earlier, Padmasambhava had pressed the edges of the two disks together with the heel of his hand, and his hand's imprint was still visible. Opening the closed stones like a jewelry box, Sodga found a container with *dakini* writing inside. The writing could be deciphered only through the boy's wisdom.

Twelve volumes of Padmasambhava's treasures were thus revealed by my stepfather on that occasion. In truth my stepfather was the incarnation of a Nyingma *terton,* though this was never officially acknowledged. He practiced both Gelugpa and Nyingma traditions and exemplified both by his unobstructed spiritual perspective.

One day while I was still living in his house, my stepfather suggested we walk to the top of a mountain named Trag-chenma, remarkable because the rock formation at the top looked like a huge ear. Inside was a cave.

"There is a *terma* here," my stepfather said as we entered the cave. He took his knife out of its sheath and plunged it directly into the stone wall of the cave. The stone offered no resistance. When he withdrew the knife, a hole remained, which he plugged with a blade-shaped piece of wood to indicate where the *terma* might be revealed in the future. He did not say one word about this incident, and when I boasted of it, no one believed me. This demonstration of his powers as a *siddha* had been for me, and me alone.

Despite the respect I accorded my stepfather, despite the utmost kindness he bestowed on me, we never developed the warm, jocular familiarity that typifies the kinship of many Tibetan fathers and sons. Our relationship was more correct than affectionate, though it had improved immensely since I had jealously tried to kill him with my bow and arrow as a child. In particular, I think he approved of my decisions to remain in three-year retreat and to offer my mother's wealth to the Vajrasattva prayer wheel.

In a deep sense, however, I knew I could rely on his love and compassion. My trust in him and my intuition that he had dealt with issues similar to mine caused me to turn to him when I began to deal seriously with my sexuality.

My sex education began during my three-year retreat when we were trained in the six yogas of Naropa. We learned the practice of inner heat and certain other yogas, but any specific reference to consort practice was censored because our teachers didn't want to jeopardize our monks' vows. However, the possibility of accomplishing the yogas with a consort certainly hovered at the periphery of my consciousness. Like most Tibetans I had seen *t'hangkas* of deities joined in sexual union, and if the specifics were still a mystery to me, the general idea was compelling.

Physical yogic practices, including consort practice, are skillful methods to master the subtle channels, winds and movement of energies through the body. The purpose of these practices is to free ordinary desire and dualistic concepts and to awaken the realization of the inseparability of one's absolute nature and great bliss. Full realization is a state of enlightened awareness.

In accomplishing the inner heat and other yogas, we were learning to visualize and direct the energies of the body. These skills stimulated my wish to know more about the yoga of consort practice. One day a visitor brought an extraordinary skullcup and a statue of the wisdom consort Dorje P'hagmo from a holy place named Tzari on the border of India and Tibet—the same Tzari to which Chagdud Tanpai Gyaltsan had tried to travel when he had been thwarted by obstacles. We placed the skullcup, which represents the container of the entire universe, on the altar and performed an offering ceremony. That night, when everyone was sleeping, I returned to the meditation hall and prayed with heartfelt aspiration. I prayed that I would be able to benefit all beings, but that I would do so as a *ngagpa,* a yogi who holds no vows of celibacy. I aspired to transcend ordinary desire and attain full realization of the inseparability of bliss and absolute nature.

Later, I told my stepfather about my prayer and my reflections on the nature of desire. "Yes, desire must be transmuted," he replied, "and this is possible through the yoga of consort practice. It is not easy. It takes masterful yogic skill to attain the fruits of consort practice. It is difficult not to deviate into ordinary desire, ordinary pleasure. Nevertheless, you should know that in your family there have been many who reached full realization of consort practice. If you could do this, it would be a great accomplishment."

I was encouraged by what he said. Eventually my high ideals might have given way, however, had I not been surrounded by my teachers and attendants whenever an encounter with an attractive young woman was possible. One night in particular my stepfather, Lama Tse Gon and I were in Bumsar staying in a large tent. Sleeping in a different section of the tent was a girl who captured my imagination. I wanted her to notice me. Thinking my stepfather and *gegan-la* were asleep, I started to throw little pebbles at her.

I don't know what I would have done had she reciprocated my flirtatious attentions, but she didn't. She pretended to be sound asleep even though my shots were becoming quite accurate. My stepfather, however, was not asleep, and the next day he gave me a stern lecture.

"Don't throw away both your monk's vows and your aspiration to be a *ngagpa* like this," he said. "You've had

Chagdud Gonpa ◆ Padma Publishing
P.O. Box 279
Junction City, CA 96048-0279
USA

place
stamp
here

some yogic training, but not enough to accomplish consort practice. If you attempt it, you may lose control and fall into ordinary, deluded desire.

"I can give you an empowerment and teaching; then we must do nine months of retreat together. If not nine, then no less than six months." It had been prophesied that my stepfather would make me the lineage holder of one of his treasures. Among the treasures he had revealed was a profound Padma Dakini practice, a method to master consort yoga. It is extremely rare to receive such a teaching, but my stepfather thought that by giving it to me he would fulfill the prophecy.

Again we went to the mountain of Tragchenma, to the cave where he had plunged his knife into rock. Again he demonstrated his powers. The empowerment into Padma Dakini practice involved constructing a wooden triangle to contain a fire and to support a metal plate. Standing a short distance away, Sodga lit a small torch as a symbolic gesture. In the same instant, the fire in the triangle flared forth spontaneously. This display deeply impressed me and I approached the practice with a certain awe.

The retreat itself was strict, strenuous and solitary. We saw no one except the attendants who brought our food. The first third of the retreat was spent in developing clear visualization and mantra recitation, the rest of the time in working with the subtle channels and winds and directing the body's male and female energies.

There are several extraordinary physical signs of full accomplishment of the Padma Dakini practice. I did not achieve these in six months, and my stepfather said they would have been accomplished more perfectly in nine. Still, my signs were quite good. My stepfather felt confident in authorizing me to do this practice, knowing that the molten streams of my youthful sexuality were now skillfully channeled and under control.

ANOTHER GREAT SERVICE my stepfather did for me during these years was to arrange an audience with Sechhen Rabjam at Sechhen Gonpa. Sechhen Rabjam lived in retreat and saw almost no one. He agreed to see me solely because I was the son of Delog Dawa Drolma and the stepson of Sodga.

When we arrived, Sodga made offerings and requested that Sechhen Rabjam determine which deity practice would be of most benefit for my development. He agreed and told us to come back in three days.

Upon our return we found displayed before Sechhen Rabjam a magnificent mandala of Green Tara, the deity of enlightened activity. He empowered me into a Green Tara practice and said, "If you do this practice to the point of realization, you will benefit countless beings."

My mother, herself an emanation of White Tara, had been the treasure discoverer of a Green Tara practice. My relationship to her was the first sign of my affinity with Tara in this lifetime. It was affirmed again and again, first by Sechhen Rabjam, then by others, that Tara, in all her wisdom aspects, would bless my practice and be a source of my benefit to others.

EVERYTHING SEEMED to be going well. Outwardly my activity alternated between reciting prayers and performing ceremonies for others, and learning and practicing meditation for my own development. Inwardly I attained new levels of understanding, greater mastery of my thoughts and emotions and a wider, more open perspective through my meditation. Secretly I was working with profound energies, the potential to realize the inseparability of absolute nature and ultimate bliss. I was self-directed and confident and at the same time the beneficiary of superb guidance.

Yet things were not perfect. Through my practice of Mahamudra I recognized the fallacy of the concept of "I," the fallacy of the ego as a reference point for reality. Mahamudra meditation brought maturity to my understanding, yet I did not experience what I had previously experienced as a child through my visions and dreams, an absolute nakedness of being. I felt like a deaf-mute who had once tasted sugar and could not repeat the experience because he had no name for it. I did not brood on it, but I could not be satisfied with less.

6

Conflict and Retreat

IN THE LATE SUMMER the monks and lamas of Tenp'hel Gonpa went on an expedition to cut grass to use as winter fodder for the horses. It was more an extended picnic than hard work because we took long breaks to drink tea and eat, then settled back on the warm earth and stared up into the zenith of the sky. As one person would begin to drift into sleep, another would wake him up with a joke or a story. Afterward, we went back to cutting the sweet-smelling grass, singing Tibetan folk songs.

In the midafternoon of the sixth day we loaded up the bundles of grass onto yaks and set out for Tenp'hel Gonpa. Because we left later than we had anticipated, we had to stay overnight at the house of a family along the way. This meant that my room in the monastery would be unattended for that night, which made me uneasy.

As I went to sleep I had a vision of two men I knew, Jampal and his brother, entering my room at the monastery and throwing the luggage out the window. I woke up angry the next morning and told people, "I think I've been robbed."

When we reached the monastery I found that my belongings, including precious ritual implements I had received from my mother, were gone. I asked an old monk, "Who came into the monastery last night?"

"Jampal and his brother were here," he replied.

I went to see the incarnation of Tulku Gyurmed Namgyal Dorje, the old lama who had been the reason for my mother moving to Tenp'hel Gonpa. He had died and reincarnated as a young boy with extraordinary powers of clairvoyance. I told him that my things had been stolen, but said nothing about my suspicions. "Can you see who took them?"

"Oh, yes," he said immediately. "Jampal stole them."

My own vision twice confirmed, I went directly to Jampal's house and demanded that he return my stolen possessions.

"How can I return them if I don't have them?" he asked. "I didn't steal your things."

I knew he was lying, and I was incensed as much by his audacious deceit as by his thievery. "I know you stole those things, I know you are lying and I know you won't get away with it," I warned, my face shaking with rage. I stormed out of his house and went back to the monastery, where I announced to the monks what had happened. I expected them to seize Jampal and force him to return my stolen things. In Tibet monks are not particularly docile, especially when someone has acted with contempt toward one of their *tulkus*. I was surprised, therefore, when instead of rallying to my cause, they fell into endless discussion.

Finally, after a day of this, word came that Jampal had run away. He had six strong brothers, which in Tibet is the seed of a military force, and under their protection had found asylum in a village of three hundred families. My things were never to resurface—perhaps in his fear of my retaliation Jampal buried them.

With unabated anger, which now extended to those who failed to support me as well as those who had protected Jampal, I decided to leave Tenp'hel Gonpa and go to my family's place in Tromt'har. I took off my monk's robes, put on more ordinary clothes and rode away. This change of clothes was reflected in my outer activity as well, and for several years I invested much of my energy in worldly activities and the study of Tibetan medicine rather than spiritual practice.

My uncle was fully trained in Tibetan medicine, and people from all over the region came to him for diagnosis and treatment. His servant gathered plants and other substances and, under his supervision, prepared many of the medicines he needed. Others were purchased from traders. From him I learned to diagnose through the reading of pulses, urine analysis, questions and observation, and to treat people with remedies and through the modification of injurious habits. Under my uncle's direction I also studied medical texts. I enjoyed this work, but when I told my uncle that perhaps I would take up medicine as my profession, he tried strongly to deter me, saying I would never have any peace, that people would call me out at all hours. His words did not really avert my interest, but at the deepest level I had already dedicated my life to the activity of a lama. In later years my medical background provided methods for alleviating the suffering of others, but the methods of the dharma were far more extensive.

Meanwhile, many disputes had arisen in Tromt'har over grazing lands, and my uncle, as the richest and most powerful man in the region, was at the center of these conflicts. I served as his negotiator. In Eastern Tibet, disputes not settled by words were usually settled by guns, for there was certainly no strong government to intervene. If anything could be said in favor of the worldly conduct of my life at that time it would be that perhaps I prevented loss of life. I was a skillful mediator and people respected the agreements that I brought about. I was gaining fame and influence throughout Tromt'har and beyond.

Not every conflict was settled peacefully, however. Once two of my uncle's fine horses were stolen. We searched the area and found them. The man who had the horses told us that he had purchased them from two men from Nyagrong. We knew these two men and knew they came from a villainous tribe, not above horse theft or worse.

For a while it seemed we could do nothing about our loss, but one day, having heard that the thieves were passing through our area, we ambushed and captured them. When we demanded that they repurchase our horses and return them, they were insolent. Just as with Jampal, I was incensed by their attitude. We took their guns and horses and sent them away. In Tromt'har the rule of reparations was three horses if you stole one, so they got off lightly.

We knew, of course, that they would be back, that the incident wouldn't simply subside. They went to their people and told them that we had robbed them; then they gathered a well-armed force of thirty men, led by a man who was a famous fighter. Their intention was not just to repay an insult, but to move into the Tromt'har region and take over the grazing lands.

I was in my tent near Tromge Gonpa when a messenger ran in with news of their approach. I saddled a horse and rode off to join my uncle and the others who were defending the region. We set up an ambush, lining up our men on both sides of a narrow valley. As the leader approached, we fired.

His horse reared and threw him, but one of the great blessings of that day was that neither he nor any other man or horse on either side was killed or wounded. We fired at close range and tried to stop one another with bullets, but we were all spared injury. I had always recited many prayers that if harmful intent toward others ever arose in my mind, I should not succeed in accomplishing any nonvirtuous course of action. Perhaps those prayers were a source of protection.

Finally, some people from other villages came between us to negotiate a truce. We had to pay the invaders something to leave, but it was not more than the thieves had to pay us. The agreement held, and the incident passed.

During all this time I had not given up my intention to punish Jampal. Using all my skills as an orator, I had marshaled a force of several hundred persons and was planning to attack him in the village where he had taken asylum. However, one day I visited Tulku Arig, a saintly lama who lived in Tromt'har and who was a Tromge relative. As I did prostrations before him, he looked at me sorrowfully, his eyes filling with tears. "Don't go this way. Whether you succeed or not there will be no benefit. It is only an obstacle to your dharma. Do practice instead."

That was all he said, but his compassion melted into my innermost heart. For a long time I wept, and as I did, the jagged ice of my hostility began to thaw. Before I left his presence that day, I resolved to go into a solitary three-year retreat immediately.

I rode down to my grandmother's black tent to collect some supplies. When I told her what I was doing, she tried to dissuade me from going until a big reunion of the Tromge clan was completed in three days' time. "There is no reason you can't wait a little." Her words held no weight with me. I knew I shouldn't delay.

I asked a servant to leave a horse tied for me, but somehow it got away. I had to walk the mile from my family's tent to Tromge Gonpa, where I was going to do the retreat. A mile is not a long walk for most, but due to years of sitting in meditation posture, since earliest childhood, I have always found walking any distance very difficult, so this was a long mile.

In the monastery they gave me a small complex of rooms, which included a room for meditation and my shrine, a tiny room for my bed and a latrine. My food was cooked in the monastery kitchen and brought to me. I went into retreat in mid-July and unexpectedly heavy snow fell for three days. Everyone labored to remove snow and search for lost animals. In my retreat house I was very comfortable, as if a thick white curtain had fallen between me and my involvements in the outer world.

MY SECOND THREE-YEAR RETREAT was an experience of profound purification. In Buddhism, enlightenment has two aspects—the mind is free of all poisons and obscuring habits, and is replete with all perfect qualities of compassion and wisdom. The removal of the last traces of stains and the opening of the treasury of mind's qualities are accomplished most quickly through the highest, most direct teachings of Tibetan Buddhism, the teachings of Great Perfection (Dzogchhen) in the Nyingma tradition.

I was determined to hear and practice these teachings; no other level of practice, no matter what extraordinary yogic powers might be achieved, could fully satisfy me. My second three-year retreat became a process by which I made myself worthy to receive such teachings.

I began my retreat by repeating the preliminary practices, including another hundred thousand full prostrations. I did the *Longchen Nyingt'hig* preliminary, one of the foundations of the Nyingma tradition, and my practice was quite diligent, especially compared with the preliminary practices I had done in my first three-year retreat. It was a pleasure to do well what as a child I had done halfheartedly.

My retreat teacher was Tromge Trungpa Rinpoche, a Great Perfection master and a Tara *siddha*. He told me, "In each generation of our family, there is one lama who fully attains the beneficial power of Tara. Your mother was the Tara *siddha* of her generation, and if you do Tara practice, I believe you will be the Tara *siddha* of yours. This would be very good."

After he told me this, I chanted one hundred thousand recitations of the long praises to the twenty-one wisdom aspects of Tara. This opened the door of my Tara practice, which would become a source of continuous inspiration and blessing.

The development of my practice went well for some months. There were no interferences from the outside, my mind was properly tuned within meditation—not too taut, not too lax—the signs were good and I wanted nothing more than to continue on the same steady course.

Then, suddenly, my anger at Jampal's having stolen my belongings surfaced again, this time in an especially pernicious form—spiritual righteousness. I thought, "To this day Jampal has not confessed and has no regret. He thinks that I have no means to rectify the situation and that the dharma is powerless against his wrongdoing. His shamelessness will influence others to go the same bad way. It is not just in my interest but in that of the dharma itself that he ought to be punished and shown that nonvirtue has consequences."

These thoughts obsessed me, and that night I began to set up a mandala to the dharma protectors to invoke their wrathful intervention in the situation with Jampal. I planned to perform a ceremony the next day, but that morning, before I could begin, a monk came into the room and announced that Tromge Trungpa Rinpoche was waiting outside. This was entirely unexpected. Tromge Trungpa came to my retreat house only when I needed teachings to continue my practice, never casually, just to chat. When he came in I offered him my seat and I sat on the floor.

He began to praise me. "Tulku, it is rare to see such a practitioner as you who is truly motivated to help sentient beings. You have studied well and you have meditated well, and this is wonderful. It will bring about great benefit to others.

"You know," he continued, "there are some black-hearted practitioners who use the dharma in the wrong way. They use the protector practices to inflict suffering on others. Certainly you are not like them. I would rather you be a common marmot killer than a perverted practitioner like that."

In Tibet a marmot killer was considered the lowest kind of person because marmots are defenseless creatures. Those who ate marmot meat smelled peculiar, and people would not invite them inside their houses or tents. I was mortified that I had verged on sinking lower than a marmot killer in Tromge Trungpa's esteem.

I said nothing about the mandala I had been setting up and

offered no more than polite formalities as he left. I was afraid that I might betray the utter dismay I felt. As soon as he was a safe distance from my house, I dismantled the mandala. In truth it had served its purpose by invoking an infallible protector—Tromge Trungpa—to show me the consequences of my own nonvirtue.

It also showed me that one must practice all the way to enlightenment, because until one is fully enlightened, obstacles can intervene. I myself had studied well under superb lamas, had done retreat and experienced signs of spiritual attainment in my meditation, yet a poisonous emotion almost resulted in a huge obstacle to further attainment. My diligence and my assiduous checking of my own mind increased. As for Jampal, thirty-five years later one of his brothers came to see me. From him I learned that Jampal had been killed by a Tibetan for collaborating with the Chinese. I told this brother that I was actually indebted to Jampal because he had caused me to enter retreat and purify my anger.

MY SECOND THREE-YEAR RETREAT was different from my first in that, being eleven years older, I was much less fascinated by the signs of practice. Visions of deities arose and I had splendid dreams, but as gratifying as these were, they were temporary riches compared with the constant revelation of mind's spontaneous perfection. Through listening to and meditating on the Great Perfection teachings I received from Tromge Trungpa, there were times when all ordinary patterns of perception were simply exhausted and I rested in uncontrived awareness.

But in the last three months of the retreat, I became so sick

I thought I might die. I could not keep any food down, and without nourishment I grew extremely weak. After a while, when things did not improve, I wrote Tromge Trungpa to ask if I should leave retreat and see a doctor. He sent a message that he thought my illness was a retreat obstacle and I should not leave. I was rather sad, but I would not go against his advice. Instead I prepared to die.

Between my meditation sessions I practiced *p'howa* in order to transfer my consciousness at the moment of death. Signs came quickly and I had a vision of Amitabha Buddha, a central focus of meditation in the particular transference practice I was doing. I also practiced Vajra Yogini *p'howa* in the event that I would be too weak to utter the mantra of transference to the pure realm of Amitabha. In Vajra Yogini *p'howa*, without saying a word, one simply transfers one's consciousness into the vast expanse of wisdom. Vajra Yogini graced my practice by appearing in a vision.

One night, in a dream, I came to a place where across the entire horizon the earth shimmered and merged with the sky. It was strange, and unfamiliar. Three or four people were there and I asked them, "What is this place?"

"This is the ocean."

"I have never seen such a place."

"It is where you will die and take rebirth as a fish."

Then, in the dream, I remembered an actual incident in my childhood. A woman who had come to visit my mother was wearing an ornament that fascinated me. I asked her where it came from and she said from a fish. I ran to the stream near our house and caught a tiny fish. Though I wasn't able to look, I managed to kill it with my little knife. When I opened it up, there was no ornament, so I went back to the house empty-handed and asked the woman why she had told me such a thing. She laughed heartily and said, "No, no. You made a mistake. This ornament comes from a fish that lives in the faraway ocean." I was only four years old, but even then I knew my mistake was far more serious than choosing the wrong kind of fish.

In the dream I thought, "Oh, no. This is what will happen because I killed that fish. Well, if I must be reborn as a fish, at least let it be a small fish so it doesn't eat other fish." With that my dream ended.

Later when I went out to the latrine in the dark early morning hours, the image of a silvery gray fish appeared. No matter which way I looked the fish was there, clear and unwavering. It didn't disappear when the sun rose, or as I went about ordinary tasks, or when I visualized other images in meditation. For days and days the fish was with me constantly, until finally I did one million recitations of the mantra *Om Mani Padme Hung,* praying for the alleviation of suffering of all beings—humans, animals and those in realms unseen. At the completion of these recitations, I dedicated the virtue of my meditation to the fish I had killed, with the wish that it find happiness and ultimate liberation. Then the fish disappeared.

Still my sickness did not go away, and I lived in a constant state of nausea, in the constant expectation of dying. Death, however, occurred elsewhere. Early one morning during the last week of my retreat, there was a knock on my door and a monk, a very good practitioner who was also in retreat, walked in the door and said abruptly, "Tromge Trungpa died last night."

I was incredulous. "He came to visit me yesterday and did not show any sign of being ill."

"He was not ill." The story as it unfolded through the

monk and others was remarkable. The day before, Tromge Trungpa had learned that Tulku Arig, who had just returned from performing death ceremonies for his own revered guru, was gravely ill. Upon hearing this Tromge Trungpa murmured, "Oh, no, it would be too great a loss for Tulku Arig to die. His long life would be so useful for others. Better someone like me." He said no more and his words made no special impact on those who heard them.

That day he went around to his students, checking up on their practice, answering their questions. When he came to me, he probed my understanding of the entire range of Great Perfection teachings, explained certain points and answered every question fully. This was somewhat unusual because our pattern was for him to give a sliver of teaching and then for me to meditate extensively. I thought it was auspicious and attributed it to the fact that I would be leaving retreat soon. When he left, he bumped his forehead to mine, the conventional farewell between lamas who respect each other as peers.

That night Tromge Trungpa invited two nuns to share the evening meal with him. "Make very good food," he told them. When they had eaten, they lit many butterlamps and meditated for a while. He questioned them about their practice and asked them if they had anything they wished to be clarified. Then he said, "Recently I had a dream of a golden sunset. Perhaps Situ Rinpoche will die soon. Those who are devoted to him will shed tears and grieve, but this shows that they do not understand. When a lama dies, he attains enlightenment and this is the time to pray for blessings, not to cry, for there is great spiritual increase in that moment."

It was late and he told the nuns to sleep in his room.

One of them, who could not sleep, noticed that Tromge Trungpa's breathing was odd, as though he were repeatedly sighing. After a while she went over to his throne to see if he was all right. His head had nodded to one side. "Rinpoche, Rinpoche!" she said softly. When he didn't respond, she shook him gently, then awakened the other nun and told her to wait while she fetched the monk. The monk came and said that Tromge Trungpa was dead. He told them not to do anything until morning.

In the morning the monk came to me. We decided that the body should not be moved for three days, and so it happened that Tromge Trungpa's cremation took place on the day I left retreat. The cremation site was on a hill high above the monastery. The sky was a perfectly clear, deep blue. Smoke rose and wafted in one direction, while high above the pyre, independent of the smoke, a little cloud formed and hovered. Within the cloud were many spheres of rainbow light.

My grandmother, who was very old at the time, did not go to the cremation. As smoke rose from the pyre, she walked out of the family tent, looked toward the cremation hill and said aloud, "I wonder if there will be rainbows." Reverently, she prostrated three times in that direction and turned back toward the tent. She took several steps and fell down, dead.

Now death ceremonies began and continued for forty-nine days, for both my grandmother and Tromge Trungpa. Such extensive offerings were made that even our family, which was then still quite prosperous, felt the strain on its resources. For me, however, these ceremonies brought good fortune.

My uncle the Tibetan doctor noticed that I was not well and asked me about my symptoms. When I described them, he said, "Don't worry, this illness is easy to remedy. Why didn't you tell me before?" He put a little medicine in meat broth, which I drank. It was the first time in months that I wasn't overwhelmed by nausea. After that I felt stronger each day until I was completely well.

At the end of the ceremonies two papers that had been used in the rituals, one on behalf of Tromge Trungpa and another on behalf of my grandmother, were taken to the unsurpassed lama Jamyang Khyentse Chhökyi Lodrö. My uncle and five other men rode to his monastery to have an audience. For Tromge Trungpa my uncle asked that the paper be incorporated into Chhökyi Lodrö's practice in such a way that all who had a connection with Tromge Trungpa would experience enhanced blessings. For my grandmother he requested that her consciousness be liberated beyond the suffering of ordinary existence.

During this audience my uncle also asked Chhökyi Lodrö whether it was time to leave Kham and move to Padma Kod on the Indian border. His concern was based on a prophecy written in a religious text that our family owned. Several hundred years before, a very great lama had foretold that when a road was built through the Powo region of Tibet, terrible times would befall the country. The people should consider the road a sign to leave everything and go to Padma Kod, a region prophesied by Padmasambhava as a safe harbor during times of upheaval.

We heard that such a road was now under construction by the Chinese. My own dreams were also very disturbing and I felt we needed to relocate to Padma Kod. Chhökyi Lodrö, however, told my uncle that perhaps the prophecy was intended for the next generation. When my uncle returned, I was surprised to learn of this response, but I did not doubt Chhökyi Lodrö. Only much later would I understand that, because my uncle had inadvertently included a Chinese collaborator in his five-man party, Chhökyi Lodrö could not have spoken freely without endangering many people. Had I known the truth then, it would have been a much clearer indication than even the road itself of the divisiveness and betrayal that would doom Tibet.

THE FIRST CHINESE AUTHORITY I encountered directly was a Chinese military officer, a Communist Party organizer, who arrived in Tromt'har prominently displaying full pride of his uniform. He organized several parties to which he invited many people of stature. At the party I attended, he took my hand and walked me outside in a friendly manner. Since he did not speak Tibetan, he enacted a little charade to communicate. First, he pointed at a dog, indicating that the dog had killed a marmot. Then he pantomimed skinning the marmot, preparing the meat and serving it to his guests. He smiled broadly as he shared his joke with me, watching for my reaction. Outwardly I showed nothing, for I knew he wanted to antagonize me. Inwardly I was sickened and concerned that this man would decide to demonstrate his contempt for our customs by serving us meat we regarded as utterly defiled.

On another occasion Chinese military officers attempted to hire me to organize mining excavations for coal and other valuable minerals in the Tromt'har region. I did not want to have anything to do with the Chinese authorities, so I apologized and said I had no time. Fortunately, I was never on the receiving end of any Chinese money.

It was through the power of money that the Chinese steadily

subverted Tibetan society. When they first arrived, they paid extravagantly in silver for the smallest favor. If they rented a horse to travel two or three miles, or if someone brought water to their campsite from the creek fifty feet away, they overpaid the service enormously. In their conduct the Chinese were friendly and accommodating and, if insulted, simply smiled and turned away. Tibetans began to think they weren't so bad, especially compared with the Central Tibetan military, which requisitioned men, horses and supplies, offered little if any compensation and tolerated no protest.

During this period I mistrusted and avoided the Chinese, but I did not see their intention so clearly that I could act decisively. Many great lamas were having signs in meditation and dreams that dark times were descending, and some warned the people to prepare to leave. My own dreams were likewise ominous. In a recurring one, I was looking over the whole of Tibet. A smoky vapor enshrouded the land and the people fell unconscious.

Despite this dream, I was reassured by the words of Jamyang Khyentse Chhökyi Lodrö; I had more faith in his statement than in my dreams. Finally I decided to reenter retreat. I moved my belongings to the house on the top of a hill where Tromge Trungpa had lived and made preparations. Just before my retreat seal had been set, Tulku Jigmed Namgyal from the Tromge monastery visited me. He was about my age, a golden-hearted, generous friend, and it was clear that he would assume a large responsibility for the welfare of the next generation of the Tromge clan.

"Tulku, I know you are entering retreat," he began, "and of course it is better if you don't delay. Still, the family relies on you. I think you should know that the death ceremonies required many large offerings and our funds are quite short. At the same time we have been offering food to many people and our barley supply is very low.

"I will do what I can to support the family," Tulku Jigmed continued, "but most people in Tromt'har are devoted to Tromge Trungpa and contributed as much as they could when he died. I have been thinking about what to do and hoped that perhaps you would consider traveling to Nyagrong.

"You have not visited Chagdud Gonpa for more than ten years, and your monks and lamas must wonder if you have abandoned them. They will certainly benefit if you return and teach, and I think it will be good for you, too. You have held this monastery for many lifetimes and you should not let your connection dwindle now.

"At the same time you will be in a position to help the family here. Barley is easy to obtain in Nyagrong, and many prosperous householders will request that you perform ceremonies. It would greatly assist us if you were to use some of the offerings you receive to purchase grain and transport it to Tromt'har."

I agreed to Tulku Jigmed's request right away, knowing that he would not lightly interfere with my retreat plans. Also, although there were areas of ambivalence in my relationships with some members of the Tromge clan, they were still my blood relatives, the family of my mother, and it would be unthinkable to deny them whatever they needed. Instead of putting a seal on my retreat, I prepared to go to Nyagrong and Chagdud Gonpa to gather and send back barley.

7

Pilgrimage

ONE DAY, after staying at Chagdud Gonpa for a while, I was visited by nineteen young monks, friends I had made during my first trip to Nyagrong who were now going on the pilgrimage to Central Tibet that was customary for Chagdud Gonpa monks. Years before, we had talked about going together.

Teasingly, I asked, "What happened to our promise to take this journey together? Are you going without me?"

They were surprised. One of them said, "We never thought you would really go with us. Of course, if you can come we would rather go with you, now or even in a year, whenever you are ready."

I hadn't even considered the possibility, but in that moment I felt a strong urge to go. "I will consider it," I told the monks. I sent a request to a very great lama, Tulku Ado, who was then in retreat, to do a divination about the journey. He sent his reply. "Don't go. Nyagla Padma Duddul achieved rainbow body. He didn't go on pilgrimage; he meditated. Milarepa also achieved enlightenment by meditating, not by pilgrimage. My advice to you is don't go. Meditate."

By asking the lama for a divination I had incurred a certain obligation to follow his advice, yet it went against my desire to go, which grew increasingly compelling as the days passed. I prayed strongly for guidance. One night, the great dharma protector Ekadzati appeared to me and said, "I am the mother of basic space and I sing to you: Time is impermanent and a dance of illusion. The merit of the red-faced ones is now in decline. Through broken commitments, a poisonous stream of impurity fills the sky. The sunlight of the Buddha doctrine is dimming. My son, do not sit here. Go to the center. Places, countries, monasteries—all are illusory cities. Cut through your clinging. Hayagriva and Vajrakilaya will guard you; the mother Arya Tara holds you like a child. Your helpers, the lotus-born regents, you will see again and again. The dharma of Great Perfection is your inheritance and will come as if from father to son. But now is the time when the devouring tiger from the east will show its power—go now beyond this obstacle, before its paw catches you in the region of Kham."

My decision was made. I prepared to leave in five days.

AS WE WERE in the full excitement of packing for the pilgrimage, one of the monks in the group and all but one member of his nine-member family were brutally murdered. They were shot in their house in a village across the valley from Chagdud Gonpa by members of a powerful family from a nearby region in some senseless feud. Only one daughter survived because she had been out searching for a lost animal at the time of the massacre. Neighbors intercepted her before she returned home and warned her to flee for her life. The merciless cruelty of this event evoked not only shock and sorrow, but also a measure of bitterness, because there was no agent of law powerful enough to bring the killers to justice.

We left Chagdud Gonpa in the shadow of the slaying, with none of the jubilation that usually marked the outset of a pilgrimage. We went to Kanze, a large market town two days away by horse. In Kanze I first saw the Chinese road and I laughed. The steady flow of traffic inching along the horizon looked like a column of pigs passing nose to tail down the road. The reality, however, was far more ominous. What I witnessed was a bumper-to-bumper stream of Chinese trucks and machinery moving into Tibet. The extent of the Chinese occupation astounded me.

By this time the Chinese were making commerce difficult for the Tibetans, prohibiting transportation for traders and their wares in Chinese trucks, the only vehicles available. Since we were not involved in commercial activity, we were able to find transportation as far as Chamdo in two large Chinese trucks. Very early one morning, nineteen of us— thirteen monks, three nuns, two laymen and I—piled on top of our luggage in the open-backed trucks for the perilous journey over Trola pass.

That day we crossed mountains more than eighteen thousand feet high on a narrow, precipitous road banked on both sides with snow higher than the trucks. Many persons, Tibetan and Chinese alike, had lost their lives on this road and we could not deny our fear. Chanting prayers strongly and continuously, we arrived at Dege Gönchhen late that night. The Chinese drivers were glad we were with them, for they said there were always fewer accidents when Tibetans were in the trucks.

The drivers went off to eat by themselves, and we found

hot water, ate *tsampa* and slept by the truck. Before dawn we resumed our journey, again traveling late into the night, leaving in the predawn and finally reaching Chamdo at sunset.

Chamdo, five hundred miles east of Lhasa, was situated on a major river. Previously the Lhasa government had used Chamdo as its main administrative and military outpost for Kham. Now the Chinese military was there in force, ready to relay troops into Central Tibet. Mao Zedong had first sent his People's Liberation Army across the mountains to conquer Chamdo in 1950, only a few months after he had consolidated his power in China. Chamdo was abandoned by the army of the Central Tibetan government and fell to the Chinese undefended.

When the Chinese troops moved into Chamdo, they initially made a point of paying fair prices or more and asserted their authority with a light hand, even freeing prisoners of war. There was guarded optimism among the Khampas about their presence, and the Chinese encouraged this hopefulness. Meanwhile, they built their military infrastructure and two major roads—including the one we were traveling, which ran across Tibet from Chengdu, China, through Chamdo to Lhasa.

In Chamdo I first encountered the bitter dregs of sectarian friction between the Gelugpa and other traditions of Tibetan Buddhism. The Gelugpa is the most recently established of the four main traditions, originating as a monastic reform movement in the early fifteenth century. Although there were doctrinal differences among the traditions, sometimes strongly disputed in formal debates, in Kham there was generally acceptance and cooperation. Since both my father and stepfather were Gelugpa lamas, my mother's family was Sakya and I was trained in both Kagyu and Nyingma traditions, any outer sectarian divisiveness would have inwardly fragmented me. I was spared this conflict until I listened to stories in Chamdo, and hearing them I felt uncomfortable and sad.

People told me that previously several monasteries housing statues of Padmasambhava and Nyingma texts were located near Chamdo, but then a Gelugpa lama named P'habong Khapa came from Central Tibet. He had contempt for the Nyingma tradition and taught that its doctrine was false and its practitioners wrongheaded. The dissension that ensued resulted in persecution, the destruction of many Nyingma texts and statues of Padmasambhava and the conversion of monasteries from Nyingma to Gelugpa. This was followed by a severe drought and famine in the region. Now, a generation later, bitterness often surfaced in conversations with Chamdo residents—bitterness focused on old sectarian grievances but oblivious to the looming Chinese storm that would soon destroy, with complete impartiality, the monasteries and texts of all four Tibetan Buddhist sects.

The Chinese road had been completed to Lhasa, but in Chamdo we left the main road and followed a route through many holy places. It was a relief to break free of the oppressive presence of the Chinese military and to wend our way through the high fir forests and meadows of the Riwoche region of Kham. Each day we covered about eight or ten miles. We camped in villages and monasteries at night, or we slept in the open. At each monastery we did prostrations, meditated, recited prayers and offered incense and butterlamps.

However, the purity of the environment and the virtue of making this pilgrimage did not produce pure, virtuous behavior in all of my monks. Several of them began their journey with a large stash of silver, but insisted on following the custom of poor Tibetan pilgrims, begging for alms along the way. These monks were not humble alms seekers, but became truculent if refused a few coins or a bit of *tsampa*. Actually, in their fierce extortion of alms, they were little better than highway robbers. I was forced to intervene in order to prevent further antagonism and possible scraps. I told them that, although they could beg, they were forbidden to contest the outcome.

Afterward I checked their bags every three days and confiscated three coins for every extra coin I found. As I enforced this policy, I never failed to find something illicit in the luggage and to exact a fine. I held to these penalties and eventually turned the proceeds over to Chagdud Gonpa. I was quite dismayed at the monks' unethical conduct and had thoughts of discontinuing my journey with them.

About a week from Chamdo, we arrived at Riwoche, the site of an ancient temple that dated back to the time of Gesar of Ling. The walls were large and sturdy, and inside, on three sides, they were lined with black paper on which the story of the Buddha and other texts were written in a beautiful gold and silver script. An arrow was embedded near the ceiling of the fourth wall, which leaned inward. It was said that Gesar shot his arrow there to prevent the wall from ever falling.

Also in Riwoche I encountered Tibetan opera for the first time. I was fascinated by the high, plaintive tones that seemed like cries to me, songs I would not have recognized as Tibetan. Adorned in elaborate robes, the singers recounted the lives of famous Tibetans such as Milarepa and sang tales of gods and goddesses.

From Riwoche we had to cross another high pass into the Powo Chung Tola region, a pass notorious for avalanches. It was said that if you were absolutely silent, the goddess of the mountain would look favorably upon you; if not, she would fling down the mountainside. We made our way across without a word, resisting the impulse to exclaim whenever partially melted snow revealed the twisted corpses and mangled carcasses of unfortunate travelers and pack animals who had provoked the fury of an avalanche.

When we were beyond the danger of the pass, I sent my monks ahead to set up camp and make tea, then I continued alone, walking slowly, hobbled by knees and hips that had been locked into meditation posture for long hours since early childhood. It was very quiet there in the high mountains without the raucous monks. After some distance my path intersected another one. A man coming down the second path walked up and fell into step with me. He was one-legged and strangely dressed in a cape of woven yak hair and a peculiar hat. His legless side was supported by a large stick, his gait a ponderous series of hops.

"Who are you and where are you going?" I asked.

"I'm a herdsman and I'm looking for a lost yak."

We went along together without talking for a while; then I asked, "Do you know the holy places of the Chung Tola region? I am with a group of monks and we are making a pilgrimage from my monastery in Nyagrong to Lhasa."

"You must go to Padma Kod," he replied. He pointed across the mountain peaks and said, "Follow this path until you come to a table rock balanced on a spire. There is a treasure there, and it will give you instructions for reaching Padma Kod.

"Tibet is in grave danger now," he continued. "It is certain that many monasteries will be destroyed and many people will die, some by a swift, sudden blow, some by slow starvation. If you don't believe what I say, return to Kham in

109

three years and you will witness the truth of my words."
Abruptly he turned toward another path, saying, "Now I must
go in a different direction." Under the sway of his words, I
stood motionless, staring at his back as he slowly made his
way down the trail. Then I went my own way to catch up
with my monks.

When I reached our camp and everyone had gathered to
drink tea, I told them about the herdsman and presented
them with the idea of going to Padma Kod. Immediately
protests fell like hail.

"It's out of the way and dangerous!"

"The road is terrible!"

"The climate there is too hot!"

"Our opportunity to see Lhasa will be lost!"

I didn't argue with the monks or try to counter their
resistance. When we continued the journey, we passed near
the table rock balanced on a spire, but I didn't insist that we
detour over to it, given their adamant stance against going to
Padma Kod. I began to ask everyone I met in the region
about the one-legged herdsman, but no one had ever seen or
heard of anyone of his description. Gradually I realized that
the encounter had not been one with an ordinary human, but
that the mysterious, prophetic herdsman had actually been
one of the guardian deities made manifest to me through an
extremely vivid and lifelike vision. I said no more about him,
but his words gave me a fierce, unshakable resolve to go to
Padma Kod.

Our next stop was Chudo Gonpa, a Gelugpa monastery,
where we saw wonderful ceremonies and lama dances. A great
stupa was part of the monastery complex, supposedly on a
site where the epic hero Gesar had entombed a demoness. A
few months before our arrival, however, a *terton,* or treasure

discoverer, had come and said that everyone had gotten the story wrong, that the demoness was buried in a different spot. This upset the people by undermining the belief they had held for many generations and they challenged the *terton*.

"So you have no faith in my words!" he replied. "Why shouldn't I know where the demoness is buried—I put her in her grave! I am the incarnation of Gesar's minister Shanpa and I was here when we put her under a big rock at a spot down near the river. You can find out whether I'm a liar by digging where I tell you." He went to the site and marked a circle twenty-five feet in diameter.

The people couldn't walk away from his dare, so muttering about this crazy lama, they started to dig. After some days of hard labor, they hit a huge stone disk that no one could move. Their skepticism having changed to excitement, they summoned the *terton*. He supervised as they wedged poles under the rock to pry it up and support it. At last they were able to retrieve the bones under the rock, the bones of a giantess whose upper arm had been more than five feet long. During Gesar's time these giants were killers who preyed on humans, and Gesar had suppressed them.

After everyone had seen the giant bones and the *terton* had made his point, the bones were placed back in the grave and the stone lowered. The *terton* went on his way, though of course the people, now in awe of his extraordinary qualities and full of devotion, begged him to stay.

When it came time for us to depart from Chudo Gonpa, I again talked about going to Padma Kod and again encountered strong resistance. This time I suggested that we part ways and I go to Padma Kod alone. Dismayed, the monks said it would be too shameful to lose their lama on their pilgrimage—we must travel to Central Tibet together and we must return to Eastern Tibet. Inwardly, I remained unswayed, but I gave up the argument and we continued on course, headed for the region of Kongpo, to a place called Tzari, where I, in my previous incarnation, had been directed to go to meditate in order to increase my longevity. Obstacles had prevented me from going, and I had died shortly thereafter at the age of twenty-eight.

En route to Tzari we had to cross a narrow, swift river. The residents of the area warned us to be quiet during the crossing, for the river's calm would correspond to our own. We followed this advice, but once on the other side, ungrateful and irreverent, we let out the blood-curdling yells Khampas make when they cross a mountain pass or ride their horses wildly into battle. Immediately the river became choppy and it rose at least a foot in the short time I stood on the bank.

When we arrived at Tzari, I told my monks that I was stopping there for a week to meditate. "One of you will stay with me to cook; the rest should continue the pilgrimage in this valley and on into Central Tibet. Then I'll catch up to you." Knowing the history of my thwarted visit to Tzari in my previous incarnation, the monks agreed to follow my instructions. They went on their way, and the young monk who had been designated as my attendant set up our camp for the night.

The next morning I told him, "Now I am going to Padma Kod. Do you want to come with me?" "Yes, Rinpoche," he replied. As we began to ride in that direction, I became very happy and at peace. That night we camped in a warm, dry cave and I fell asleep in a state of deep satisfaction, which dissipated at dawn when I discovered that my attendant had run off to alert the other monks. It disappeared altogether that day when a man from Tzari came to complain that one of my monks had stolen a valuable necklace of turquoise and coral and asked me to help get it back.

My monks found me in a dangerous temper. At first, all of them denied the theft, which infuriated me so much that the culprit, the youngest monk in the group, confessed just as I was about to tear through everyone's luggage until the necklace was found. Digging through his luggage he fished out the necklace and, not meeting my eyes, handed it to me to return to its owner.

Gradually my anger subsided, but I felt deeply discouraged. The bonds between me and my monks were very strong, based on both spiritual and social ties. In one sense I regarded them as my spiritual children, even though I was only twenty-five and several of them were as old as I or older. Just as parents see the good qualities and faults of their children and do not abandon their children when faults seem to prevail, I could not leave these monks. As long as they relied on me as their lama, I was obligated to use whatever skillful means I had to tame their minds.

I also had to consider the obligations I had to their families. People in the villages around Chagdud Gonpa trusted me to train their sons, counsel their families and uphold the social ties that had been formed over many generations and, for me as a *tulku*, over many lifetimes of consciously taking rebirths that would reestablish my connection to the Gonpa and its lay community. If I were to chastise the monks or break with them in a way that disgraced their families, it would cause divisiveness and more harm than benefit, yet I must enforce the moral discipline that is the foundation of monastic training. At the deepest level I recognized that the heart connection between a lama and a real disciple had not yet ripened between me and any one of these monks. They respected and were devoted to me and thought me a worthy leader, but they were not ready to make their minds truly responsive to my guidance. I knew this because I myself had experienced the surrender of my self-willed direction to the guidance of my own lamas on many occasions. My lamas did not have to cajole me or convince me of the wisdom of their wishes. For example, when Tulku Arig had told me to drop my worldly course of action and do practice, it was as though the powerful pulse of his pure heart had synchronized itself with my own heart's pulse. Nothing within me could possibly have contradicted him; I went straight into retreat.

Now once more I was lecturing my monks on the bad results their stealing and rowdy conduct would bring, telling them I would rather not travel with them, telling them I had chosen to go to Padma Kod. Once more they were promising to refrain from stealing, promising to conduct themselves well, imploring me to continue with them to Lhasa. And, once more, we traveled on together, though I knew nothing had been resolved.

WE WERE IN THE REGION of Yarlung and went to the Shelgrak crystal cave, which held a famous statue of Padmasambhava that had been made during his lifetime. Padmasambhava himself had declared the image an accurate likeness, so I was fascinated to see it.

Not far from the cave at Tradrug monastery was a very holy statue of Tara, one famous for its ability to speak. We did Tara practice in the shrineroom there; then, as we were leaving, I heard a high, feeble voice calling, "Lama! Lama!" I looked back and saw an ancient nun running toward me as fast as her old legs would carry her. When she caught up, she pointed to the west and said, "I am going there and I'll meet you." I must have looked baffled because she pointed west again and said, "I'll meet you there." With that she turned around and left. I still didn't know what she meant, but she was so definite that the encounter stayed in my mind. I would meet her twenty-five years later, when she became my student in the United States and, eventually, my interpreter.

At last we reached Mindroling Gonpa, a renowned monastery in Drachi that had a branch in Eastern Tibet one day's ride from Chagdud Gonpa. For me arriving at Mindroling was like coming home. I knew many of the lamas, I knew the practices done there, I knew the style of chanting and I knew, with complete certainty, that I was going to stay there for a while. My monks protested, and finding no way to breach my resolve this time, they appealed to the abbot of the monastery, who was also the regent of the young spiritual heir to the dharma seat, Mindroling Khanchhen. To their dismay, he supported me. "Let the lama stay and do his dharma activity in the way he sees is best to create benefit for sentient beings. You finish your pilgrimage; then, when you return to your monastery, send several attendants to the lama."

The monks were sorrowful. I summoned them and talked to them very seriously. "You need to listen to what I say and follow my advice," I began. "Now you are going on without me. I guarantee your safe passage if you don't fight and don't steal, but I also know big trouble will surely befall you if you continue with your bad behavior. Something is wrong. I will pray, but you must really listen this time and do as I say."

For a month after they left I received instruction from Mindroling Khanchhen Rinpoche, a great scholar. One day during this period, I heard terrible news of my monks. They had gone to Lhasa and to nearby holy places and, along the way, had begged alms. One day a conflict flared up between them and some people who had refused them alms or given very little. These people would not tolerate the monks' aggressive demands, and in the fight that ensued, the youngest monk—the one who had stolen the necklace in Tzari—was stabbed to death and a layman was critically wounded. Afterward, the monks changed their ways and returned to Chagdud Gonpa without incident.

I performed *p'howa* for the monk who had died and prayed strongly for the safety of the others. I deeply regretted what had happened and felt a certain loneliness in being apart from my monks. More than at any time in my life I was separated from my family, friends and monastery, without attendants or even a horse. Yet despite the underlying loneliness, there was pleasure in being free to make decisions alone, without having to discuss them with others or having to consider the effect of every move on those around me. These circumstances would not last long, but momentarily I enjoyed my independence. I decided to make a pilgrimage to Samye, Padmasambhava's own monastery, and follow it with a retreat in the caves nearby.

8

My Lama

MINDROLING KHANCHHEN RINPOCHE advised me about my journey to Samye and the retreat I planned to make in one of the caves near the monastery. "You are welcome to borrow one of the monastery's horses," he said.

"Thank you, but after walking all the way from Kham, I should be strong enough to cover the three hours from Mindroling to Samye. I will leave most of my gear here and carry only a few supplies. I will buy the rest of my food there."

"Oh, no, you must not take much money. The region is notorious for its robbers, and occasionally they kill people. Anyway, there is almost no food to purchase in the area. Don't worry about support for your retreat. I know a generous sponsor who lives in the area and who will be glad to send supplies to you."

As soon as I set out for Samye, I realized that it had been a mistake to turn down the offer of a horse and not to reckon with the burden of even a small pack of supplies. It took me two days to cover the distance anyone else could have covered in an hour. I would walk slowly for a little while and rest, walk and rest. Toward evening I came to a settlement near a river I would have to cross the next day. The sponsor mentioned by Mindroling Khanchhen lived in this settlement, but I didn't want to walk up to his door and ask favors. Instead I went to the home of a very poor man and asked if I could stay overnight.

"You can stay, but you can't come in the house," he replied. "A lot of thieves put on lamas' robes, then steal whatever they want when they get inside." So I sat in front of his door, and after a while he brought me a bowl of soup, for which I was very grateful. After drinking it, I started to do my practice. Then my host understood that I really was a lama and, after tidying up his little house, invited me in to sleep. Exhausted from walking, I slept soundly.

In the morning I walked down to the river's edge, where I met another Khampa lama. We shared a ferry across the river, and on the other side we fell in together because he, too, was a slow walker. That night we slept at Zungkar Gonpa, which was remarkable for its five *stupas*, carved out of solid rock.

Finally, on the third morning after I left Mindroling Gonpa, we found ourselves on a ridge, gazing across a deep valley at Samye. The road skirted the edge of the valley, so I turned to my companion, whose name was Naygo Lama, and suggested that we leave the road and cut directly across the valley.

"I don't think it's a good idea," he replied. "There must be a sensible reason that others before us have taken the long route."

"Good idea or not," I said, "I am going straight across. We can meet again at Samye." We each went our own way and I quickly found out why the path didn't run directly to the monastery. The valley was full of sand, which made every step a struggle. At last, however, I came to the western gate of Samye and stood awestruck before a fifteen-foot statue of Hayagriva, the wrathful emanation of Buddha Amitabha. The auspiciousness of having arrived at the western gate via the direct route overrode any regret at the difficulty of the walk. The statue had been made during the time of Padmasambhava, sponsored by King Trisong Detsen, and when it was consecrated the green horse head that juts from Hayagriva's head actually neighed.

I went inside and asked the shrinekeeper if I might stay in the shrineroom for a few days. Very good-heartedly he said that I could stay as long as I was willing to step outside with my luggage when the guards made their evening rounds.

The next day I heard that Jigdral Yeshe Dorje, that is, His Holiness Dudjom Rinpoche, one of the great lamas of the Nyingma lineage, would be giving the empowerments of the Rinchhen Terdzod, a collection of practices revealed by various *tertons*. Feeling extremely fortunate, I went to the site of the empowerments. I entered during the break and approached His Holiness to offer him a long blue *katag*.

"Who are you?" he asked. "Have we met before?" He spoke softly in a Central Tibetan accent, and he was very refined in appearance.

"I am Chagdud Tulku of Chagdud Gonpa in Nyagrong and my mother was Delog Dawa Drolma."

"Oh, I knew your mother!" he exclaimed, and he invited me to visit him in his residential quarters the next day. Upon my arrival he introduced me to his wife, Sangyum Kushog Rigdzin Wangmo, as the son of Delog Dawa Drolma. The *sangyum* immediately stood up, walked over to the table of food offerings, or *tsog*, took a plate of sweet *tsampa* that was beautifully sculpted and brought it to me. As I received it I felt that this was indeed a momentous occasion, and the *tsog* sustained me for several days while I took the empowerments. During this period at Samye, I also met His Holiness's son, Thinley Norbu Rinpoche.

However, I was getting short of food, and having brought almost no money, I decided to enter retreat immediately while I still had the wherewithal to do so. I hoped that supplies would arrive soon from my sponsor. I left Samye for the nearby caves of Chenpu and established retreat boundaries around one of the caves, making a commitment to stay in retreat for one month to complete a longevity practice.

For each of the first four days I had a small ball of *tsampa;* on the fifth day I decided to divide the ball into four pieces and add them to soup for four more days. Then my food was gone, but my practice was very clear and strong. That night I had the first of a series of dreams about the dharma protectors. They presented themselves in their full power and glory and assured me that they would find food for me, that I should practice without concern.

The next morning there was a knock, and when I went outside I found that someone had left an offering of a bit of tea and a dab of butter. The disparity between the amazing dream and the tiny offering made it clear to me that I somehow lacked merit. I realized that I was going to have to deal with hunger during this retreat, because without merit there would be no way for the dharma protectors or anyone else to manifest a wealth of sustenance for me. The irony of doing long-life practice while starving to death was not lost on me.

That night I had another reassuring dream of the dharma protectors. "Certainly we are bringing you food. Do not worry." In the morning there came a knock, and outside I found seven small potatoes. I ate one each day, and when they were gone I had another dream and received a little *tsampa* the next morning. My body was very weak by now, and once this last *tsampa* was gone, and no knock and no offering followed it, starvation seemed imminent. That morning, however, a lama came to visit me.

"I am in a nearby cave doing a three-year retreat to recite the long-life prayer of His Holiness the Dalai Lama. I heard there was a Khampa lama here and thought I would like to make your acquaintance."

I invited him in and we chatted. After a while he said, "It's time for your lunch, so I should be on my way."

"Don't worry about my lunch," I said. "I have no food so I won't have any lunch."

My visitor was quite surprised. I explained that my sponsor had failed to send supplies and that I had left my money at Mindroling Gonpa. The lama left and came back to cook for me. He made a soup with wheat dumplings and a bit of meat—a meal I truly enjoyed. For several days after that he prepared a daily meal for me. Then, unexpectedly, supplies arrived from my sponsor along with a note expressing great regret that he had forgotten about me. When he remembered, he went immediately to Mindroling and learned that I had left more than three weeks before. He sent an abundance of *tsampa*, which I was able to share with any poor people who passed my cave. I now had more than enough provisions to complete my retreat commitment.

Walking back to Samye from the caves, I met Naygo Lama, who also had just completed a retreat, and together we visited the meditation cave of Gyalwa Chhogyang, one of the twenty-five disciples of Padmasambhava. In *t'hangkas* Gyalwa Chhogyang is always represented with Hayagriva's green horse head jutting from his crown. Though his cave was usually locked, we were fortunate to find the door open and we spent the night there. It was an extraordinary cave, perfectly hollowed out, the stone completely smooth. When we awakened the next morning, we found liquid shimmering down the walls of the cave. Since there was no source, Naygo and I perceived it as wisdom nectar and took it as the blessing of our retreats.

When I returned to Samye, His Holiness Dudjom Rinpoche was just completing the oral transmission of the *Dzod Dun*, the famous *Seven Treasures* of Longchenpa. I arrived in time to hear the last half of the last text and to participate in a great offering ceremony. Having come at the end of ceremonies that had been taking place for many weeks, I had no established seat and sat in one of the back rows. At one point everyone stood, and so that I could see over the crowd, I stepped on a cushion.

"Get off that cushion!"

I whipped around to see who dared order me around so rudely and found myself face-to-face with a pugnacious-looking monk. Furious, I drew back my fist to land a punch. Fortunately, an inner restraint took hold and I dropped my hand. I was instantaneously flooded with remorse as I realized how disastrous it would be to hit a sangha member in a holy place like Samye in the presence of Dudjom Rinpoche. Silently I invoked the wisdom beings and confessed my mistake with genuine regret, praying that it would be purified by wisdom light and nectar. This incident did not simply wash out of my mind, however, and afterward during offering ceremonies I would often remember with deep remorse how close my temper had brought me to disgrace.

The next morning His Holiness led a great procession of eight hundred people around Samye, and all the monastery's treasures were displayed to him. I arrived early and established my place in the ranks of lamas, close behind Dudjom Rinpoche, and therefore had a good view of these sacred objects. Even more remarkable than the objects was the oracle of Samye. From behind a partition in the second-story courtyard of the central building appeared an ordinary man. Suddenly, with a terrifying cry, he fainted. When he regained consciousness, his body was taken over by the powerful, fierce dharma protector Tzimara, his face contorted and red, his speech guttural and his language strange. With a low, sweeping bow he indicated that His Holiness should be seated on a high throne; the oracle then sat on a low chair beside him. An attendant brought a splendid golden cup filled with consecrated whiskey to the oracle, who snatched it away and turned reverently toward His Holiness to offer it to him. After taking a sip, His Holiness offered the cup back to the oracle, who downed the drink in a single, fiery gulp. Then the oracle spoke, his words indecipherable to me, but not to everyone.

Finally, he escorted His Holiness to a column in the center of the room where some object—said by some to be a mask—was enshrouded in cloth. The oracle held back the cloth so that only His Holiness could see inside; then, letting the cloth drop back, he fell unconscious again. Color drained from his face, strength from his body, and when he came to, it was as an ordinary man, so weak that he had to be supported as he left the room.

After participating in these activities, I returned to the caves of Chenpu and did two more months of retreat, as did Naygo

Lama. When we completed our retreats, we journeyed together to Lhasa.

THE FIRST NIGHT in Lhasa, Naygo Lama and I stayed in the
house of a friend of his from Kham. We went to the Jowo
shrine and meditated in the presence of the famous statue
there. On the way back I got thoroughly lost in Lhasa's maze
of back streets and alleys until, remembering the name of the
house next to ours, I got directions back. The next day I went
to the house of Pomda Tsang, one of Tulku Arig's disciples,
and asked him if I could stay there.

"Right now our guest room is being occupied by Khanpo
Dorje," he replied, "but I will go ask the *khanpo* if you may
sleep on a spare bed in the room." He left and a few minutes
later returned to tell me that Khanpo Dorje had agreed to
this arrangement.

I could not have been more delighted. Khanpo Dorje was a
very famous scholar and meditator and, like Tulku Arig, a
student of Khanpo Ngaga. For me, the opportunity to stay in
the presence of this great lama was supremely auspicious.

Yet our first meeting consisted of a lesson in the ordinary.
The lady of the house, Cham Padmala, greeted me and
showed me to the guest room, where Khanpo Dorje and I
were introduced. She then had a servant bring us tea. Now in
Eastern Tibet, you would drink some tea and the cup would
be instantly refilled, and you would drink some more and it
would be refilled, and so on until you indicated that you had
had enough tea by emptying the cup and licking it clean.

On this assumption, I accepted tea from the servant, who
waited for a moment, then disappeared for a half hour. In the

124

interim I decided that I was going to be offered only one cup of tea and no refills—an unforgivable breach of etiquette in Kham—so I drank my tea and licked my cup clean. To my surprise the servant returned, refilled our cups, waited and disappeared again.

This time, before I could drink, Khanpo Dorje spoke. "The custom of tea drinking in Central Tibet is different from our Khampa custom." He had come from Kham to Lhasa seven or eight years before. "When you first receive your tea, you don't drink it. The servant leaves and when the servant returns, you gently blow back the butter and drink half the tea. The servant refills the tea and again goes away. When the servant comes back, you blow the butter, drink half of the tea down, and your cup will be refilled. Each time the servant comes you repeat the process. When you want no more, you drink all the tea, but you never, never lick the cup clean."

Afterward, when I had become a member of the household, the family often teased me about my arrival and how I had licked the cup clean.

I stayed on for about one year and was able to hear Khanpo Dorje teach every day. His quality as a teacher was incomparable, based on a wealth of knowledge and meditative experience. He had done twelve years of solitary retreat. The integrity of his practice is exemplified by a story. He had been in retreat for three years and had attained many extraordinary signs of accomplishment—visions, clairvoyance, auspicious dreams and realization of the true nature of the material world, whose laws no longer had power over him. Yet surveying his mind with relentless honesty, he was dissatisfied with the emotional and intellectual patterns he discerned. He left retreat and went to receive the Great

125

Perfection teachings on the nature of mind once more, this time from Khanpo Ngaga. Then he returned to retreat to actualize fully what he had heard, and he was satisfied.

Khanpo Dorje's kindness to me was immeasurable. I relied on his transmission to ignite my own realization of mind's essence, and that transmission was infallible—profound beyond the limits of words, subtle and, finally, utterly simple, like absolute mind itself.

One day we went for a walk together through the streets of Lhasa to an old cremation ground. This ground had been overtaken by houses, but in one of the yards stood a large, flat stone where previously the flesh of corpses had been chopped into small pieces and fed to the vultures as an offering. Khanpo Dorje sat down on it and said, "Tulku, go get some *chang.*" *Chang* is Tibetan beer.

I went to the *chang* shop, bought a big container and brought it back. Khanpo Dorje pulled a small cup from his *chuba,* I filled it and he drank it down. I filled his cup again and he offered the *chang* to me. Out of respect, I did not put his cup to my lips, but rather poured the *chang* into my palm and drank it. It was the first taste of *chang* I had had since my three-year retreat in Tromt'har and it tasted good—inseparable from the goodness, the perfect completion, of that moment of drinking the offering from my lama's cup.

"RINPOCHE, do you think there is any chance now of reversing the hold the Chinese have on our people?" For some time I had been thinking carefully about what action we should take concerning the Chinese occupation, and now I wanted to open the subject with Khanpo Dorje.

"No," he replied. "I think that certainly it is now too late to reverse it. Eight or nine years ago there might have been hope. Several great lamas gave advice about what was needed to avert obstacles from without and to overcome disunity from within. But their advice was ignored. There will be much suffering among the people."

"You don't believe that the Central Tibetan government will be able to maintain a negotiated peace?"

"No. Do you?"

"No. I think the Chinese have eaten half their meal and are digesting it before they eat the rest. I think the Lhasa government has ignored the devouring of Kham and is blind to the fact that Central Tibet is to be eaten next." I stopped before the anger and frustration I felt became completely apparent to my teacher. He had seen it anyway.

"Everything always shows on your face," he commented. "This habit of yours won't make things easier for you. It would be better if you could change it." Then he asked what I thought we should do.

"I think we should relocate to Padma Kod." I had never forgotten my encounter with the mysterious one-legged man on the mountain pass and his urging me to go to Padma Kod, nor my family's text, which contained Padmasambhava's prophecy, revealed by a *terton*, that in dark times Padma Kod would be a sanctuary.

Khanpo Dorje pointed out that it would not be easy to settle in an uninhabited place like Padma Kod and that he was too old to help with such an undertaking. At the time he was over seventy. He asked if I would be willing to make the arrangements myself. I told him that I would, that going to Padma Kod seemed to be our best chance of finding good conditions in Tibet and that I would start preparations immediately. Khanpo Dorje agreed to this plan.

127

It was early in 1957 and war was already raging between the Chinese and Khampas in Eastern Tibet. Refugees arrived in Central Tibet daily with horrifying accounts of villages being strafed, of brutal Chinese tribunals that conducted hellish public tortures and executions, of monks slaughtered while defending their lamas and lamas murdered while their monasteries were destroyed.

The uneasy truce that existed in Kham after the initial Chinese invasion in 1950 had disintegrated in 1955, just after I left on pilgrimage. Their roads complete and their garrisons firmly established, the Chinese dropped their sham policy of accommodation and embarked on the replacement of traditional lay and monastic structures with communist systems. Their methods were ruthless. To shatter the social structure, they introduced communist "struggle sessions" in which high families were publicly accused and tortured until they confessed "crimes against the people," then were executed. They abducted thousands of children for education in their schools, and they attempted to dominate the monasteries. This restructuring was met by open, violent resistance.

The warriors of the Khampa clans, lacking unity during the invasion of 1950, rose up as an organized guerrilla force in late 1955, overwhelming Chinese garrisons in Dege, Kanze, Nyagrong and other major posts. However, their new roads and their airstrips in Chamdo and Kanze made it possible for the Chinese to reinforce their troops easily. The retreat of the Chinese garrisons in 1955 did not signal defeat. It signaled a bloody escalation of conflict.

In Lhasa the plight of Kham was generally considered of the Khampas' own making because, it was said, Khampas knew only how to fight and not how to negotiate. The implication of the Chinese devastation of village, regional and monastic structures in Kham was ignored. Ignored as well were the thousands of Chinese troops camped on the outskirts of Lhasa, the significance of the Chinese roads as arteries for military supplies and the subversion of the Central Tibetan government by an administrative committee fabricated by the Chinese to expound their own self-interested policies. The Central Tibetan government had become powerless, and the Chinese simply bypassed it.

There was much talk about political maneuvers in those days of political disintegration. I rarely participated. No matter how carefully I chose my words, my feelings, as Khanpo Dorje had pointed out, would show on my face.

KHANPO DORJE had many books, statues and other precious religious artifacts to move. I packed and arranged for some of them to be transported to Kongpo, which was a day's journey by truck. Southeast of Lhasa and north of Padma Kod, Kongpo is a heavily forested, mountainous region divided by the great Tsangpo River. The Tsangpo flows eastward hundreds of miles across the Tibetan plateau before it cuts south into India, where it is known as the Brahmaputra. Having no bridge it remained a natural barrier to major troop movements, and for a time provided protection on its south side to Tibetans who were preparing to resettle or to flee.

As I arrived in Kongpo, I noticed camps of uprooted Khampas. Their presence in Kongpo, I learned, made both the local population and the Chinese military uneasy. Throughout Tibet, Khampas had a reputation for being wild and inclined to banditry, despite their qualities of courage, loyalty, cheerfulness and faith. With the Chinese they had a reputation for being ferocious fighters in war and untamable in peace.

On the south side of the Tsangpo I found a small retreat house on a mountainside. I repaired and enlarged it in anticipation of Khanpo Dorje's arrival, then did a sixteen-day *nyung-nay*, a purification practice that required total fasting, including no drinking of liquids, every other day.

Before I left Lhasa I had suggested to Khanpo Dorje that my time in Kongpo might be well spent in retreat. To this he responded, "It is not the time for you to do retreat. Now you must teach, because the teachings of the Buddha are what will most benefit people in the difficult times to come." With this in mind I began to travel out from my retreat house to teach, give empowerments and perform ceremonies.

As winter approached, another lama, Kham Wang Tulku, and I undertook a Vajrakilaya *drubchhen,* or practice of "great accomplishment." The meditational deity Vajrakilaya is a wrathful expression of compassion and wisdom. The practitioner adopts the indomitable attitude of Vajrakilaya and uses the skills of meditation and ritual to purify completely the poisons of anger, grasping, ignorance, jealousy and pride. When these inner poisons are removed, their outer reflections as enemies, illness and the bad circumstances of ordinary existence are also removed.

At that time, as the Tibetans were confronted by the Chinese military, those of us who were lamas needed to bring the methods of purification to as many people as possible. We did not hold out hope that the violent conflict that had swept through Eastern Tibet and was overtaking Lhasa could now be averted in Kongpo by religious ceremonies, no matter how great. Rather we hoped that for the people participating in the ceremonies, the karmic causes for experiencing violence would be purified. We hoped that they would be able to deal with the hostile forces of war skillfully, without giving rise to hatred. We hoped that the virtue generated in the ceremony would protect them, but that if death came they would find liberation.

Khanpo Dorje arrived from Lhasa after the Vajrakilaya ceremony and stayed with me in my retreat house for the next six months. That first year and a half in Kongpo was deeply satisfying. It marked a time when I was able to serve the people and my revered lama, and it was, in that region, a time of relative peace and cultural and religious integrity.

In the spring Kham Wang Tulku, three other lamas and I organized a Guru Rinpoche *drubchhen* that was attended by several hundred people. Together we recited ten million Guru Rinpoche mantras. Although it was not apparent at the time, this large ceremony marked a turning point for me and the other four lamas. The Chinese feared our ability to assemble so many people. They did not believe that our motivation was purely religious and were paranoid about our organizing political or military resistance. They did not act on their paranoia immediately, but when they did, I and the other lamas would have to live like foxes evading hunters.

IN THE EARLY SPRING of 1958, while snow was still deep in the mountains, I went with seven other men to explore Padma Kod and make a plan to relocate or escape, whichever would be necessary. Padma Kod lay south of Kongpo, across high Himalayan passes. It had always been an underpopulated region with many uninhabited valleys and deep forests that became jungles near the Indian border. Now, however, people were beginning to resettle there, hoping to avoid the Chinese occupation but still live within Tibet.

Because of the time of year, avalanches were a grave danger, and many people warned us not to go. Finally I said that I would look for signs in my dreams. A night or two later I dreamed that I came upon two lakes and a rock shaped like a long-life vase, which seemed very auspicious. The next day I asked some hunters if they had ever come across natural features like these. They said that they knew of a trail through the mountains that cut between two lakes, but they had never come across a rock like the one I described.

Everyone felt that it would be safe enough crossing the pass by this trail, so we set out. Another lama, Kat'hog Ontrul Rinpoche, went on the expedition. He was very strong and carried a big load. The others also carried large loads. I, hindered by my lifelong inability to walk well, carried only a sleeping roll.

The snow was fifteen to twenty feet deep, and the tops of trees looked like little bushes sticking out of the ground. We passed through terrain with two lakes and were going over a long, icy slope. There, even my sleeping roll seemed burdensome, so I took it off and shoved it down the slope, calculating that it would slide along the mountain's natural curve and fall near our path below. Instead, it veered at a completely different angle and disappeared over a cliff. There was a somewhat exasperated silence. Probably half our group was wondering why I had tossed my gear away and half was wondering what to do about it. Then someone said, "Let's keep going down the trail. There's a ledge below and we can make tea and figure out what to do."

The trail curved sharply, and from the ledge we had a full

view of the cliff. While the others busied themselves gathering wood for a fire and preparing tea, one man and I scanned the cliff for my sleeping roll. Suddenly he shouted, "Tulku, I see it!" I followed his line of sight and was astonished to see jutting out of the cliff a rock with a striking resemblance to a long-life vase—the rock in my dream.

From the top of the rock trickled a tiny spring, and near the spring grew a sapling. My sleeping roll was snagged in its branches. With effort we made a branch mat across the snow and, using ropes to support ourselves, climbed across the cliff and up the rock to retrieve the sleeping roll. It was so encouraging to see the long-life rock that I felt justified in the inconvenience I had caused.

In Padma Kod we found an uninhabited valley that would be suitable for settlement, then trekked back across the mountains uneventfully.

MANY KONGPO PEOPLE had pointed out to me that in Padma Kod there would be no monks to help carry out my dharma activity and I would need the help of a wife. I had formally given back my monk's vows to Khanpo Dorje. In Tibetan Buddhism one can return unbroken vows to the lama from whom one received them. In my case this would have been Tulku Arig, who reinstated my vows during my second three-year retreat. However, in view of the impossibility of returning to Tromt'har to do this, it was appropriate to return them to Khanpo Dorje as my root teacher.

While I was still a monk I had encountered two women with the qualities to be a spiritual consort in the highest sense. One was the daughter in a family who had asked me to perform ceremonies in their home. This young woman was quite plain in appearance, but when she served me tea in a small bowl, the tips of her middle fingers lightly touched mine. Instantly, ordinary perception subsided and I experienced the absolute nature of reality for several minutes. I had a similar experience in the presence of another woman in Lhasa. However, my being a monk and other circumstances prevented me from approaching either of these women, and these experiences never happened again.

About the time of the extensive Guru Rinpoche ceremony in the spring, a friend suggested that I call on the father of a certain well-respected Kongpo family and ask for the hand of one of his four fine daughters. After much discussion with my friend about the character of the family and my prospects for success, I went, taking a horse as a gift to the father. He accepted on behalf of his daughter Karma Drolma.

In Tibet almost all marriages were arranged by parents for their children, or at least by parents for their daughters. A suitor for a young woman might approach her father directly as I had done. My success with Karma Drolma's father was partly due to my stature as a lama, marriageable lamas being considered good prospects by many Tibetans. However the arrangements were made, marriage was considered a strong alliance of relatives and a very pragmatic matter, socially and economically. The character of the family remained a primary consideration.

My family in Tromt'har and Karma's family in Kongpo were equally well respected, and both families had produced many high lamas. Her parents were very fine people, her mother the daughter of a lama. I liked the fact that the whole family worked hard, even in the fields alongside the servants, and that they made no ostentatious display of wealth. In this respect, they were similar to my own family. I had not been comfortable with the women of Lhasa high families, who always wore brocades and ordered servants around.

Karma's father told me that the ceremony should be held on the auspicious tenth day of the lunar sixth month—in August 1958. When these arrangements were made, I told Khanpo Dorje about them and he said, "Oh, good! This is all very good!" Soon after, he went back to Lhasa to conclude his affairs.

My marriage was to be a big celebration, and *chang* was brewed in quantity. A few days before the wedding, however, some people from a village a day's ride from Karma's village asked me to perform a fire offering ceremony to alleviate a long drought. This ceremony was to be held on the shore of a lake, and as I rode to the site, escorted by a small group of monks and people from the village, I began to feel quite sick. Finally, I couldn't ride any further so I told my companions to leave me by the trail and continue on to the ceremony without me. I gave them a contribution for the substances that would be used in the fire ceremony—grains, jewels, butter and so forth—and told them that while they made the fire offerings, I would carry out the other aspects of the ritual where I waited. By this time I was shuddering uncontrollably with severe chills, but as I had promised, I performed the ritual.

After some hours they returned. As we rode home a torrential rain came, and ironically, although we had come to pray for rain, we were unequipped for it. All of us were drenched to the skin, and I became very sick indeed. A rash covered my body, probably chicken pox, and I burned with fever. I knew I had a contagious disease, and not wanting to infect the people of Karma's family and village, I sent word that I would not be able to attend the marriage celebration.

As soon as I recovered, I planned to go to Karma's home, about a day and a half from where I was living. However, I received a message that Khanpo Dorje had returned to Kongpo from Lhasa. He had settled a day's journey away in the opposite direction, so I decided to visit him first before I left for distant parts. As it turned out, it would be many months before I would meet my intended bride, and when I did I would not be a groom of good prospects, but a fugitive from executioners.

KHANPO DORJE'S BUSINESS in Lhasa had taken longer than he had expected and in the interval the Chinese had tightened their grip on the city, making it difficult for him to leave. When he finally reached Kongpo, he settled inconspicuously in a mountain forest on the north side of the Tsangpo River and minimized his outer dharma activities to avoid attracting the attention of the Chinese military. The military was reinforcing its ranks on the north side, but kept its true strength hidden. Its presence, oppressive and dangerous, like a great predator lurking in the dusk, was evident in random arrests and increasingly frequent incidents of violence.

Three Khampa friends decided to go with me to visit Khanpo Dorje. However, on the day we were to leave together, I woke up in such a black mood that I didn't even want them to see my face. I pretended to sleep, and when they couldn't rouse me out of bed, they decided I was sick and left without me. Once they were gone I began to feel much better. I had breakfast, packed and set out accompanied by one attendant.

We traveled east along the river, left my horse with a family that lived near the boat landing, then crossed to the north bank. When I arrived at Khanpo Dorje's house, the three acquaintances were already there. Despite the strong, unexplained aversion I had experienced in the morning, I felt no personal animosity toward any of them. Mainly, I was extremely happy to see Khanpo Dorje again, happy he was safely out of Lhasa and settled in Kongpo, where I would be able to help him in an emergency.

The news he brought was bleak. The fighting had reached Central Tibet within a few miles of Lhasa. The thin facade of Chinese accommodation had been shattered, and the invaders were obviously ready to force every claim to power. There was no way to predict at what time or over which issue the Chinese would break their restraint and unleash the full fury of their military might, but this seemed inevitable.

From my side, too, the news was not good. The Khampa refugees in Kongpo were unpopular with the local populace. Some of them were rude and demanding about food and shelter, and there had been incidents of theft. Several Kongpo people had complained to the Chinese authorities, and the Chinese, delighted to have an excuse, had begun to round up Khampas indiscriminately. Khanpo and I were both Khampas, and Khampa lamas were at special risk because the Chinese feared their ability to galvanize their kinsmen's resistance. There were also rumors that the Chinese wanted me particularly because of my part in bringing about the Guru Rinpoche *drubchhen* five months earlier. I wanted to resettle in Padma Kod immediately but Khanpo Dorje said no, we would wait, so we made no specific plans. He didn't explain his reason for the delay to me, and though inwardly I felt a certain dismay, my faith in his wisdom was such that I didn't insist.

On the afternoon of the third day of my visit, I walked to a nearby monastery and laid a white *katag* before the image of each dharma protector. From my heart I prayed for protection—that in these dark times the light of dharma not be extinguished, that my own spiritual qualities not deteriorate in the face of oppression and violence, that the benefit of my precious lama and the other realization holders not be lost to humankind, that the Tibetan people not be destroyed by death and delusion.

A profound calm came over me. The conflict with the Chinese, fear for my relatives in Kham, my interactions with people, my marriage, my anxiety about Khanpo Dorje, the threat of capture, Tibet itself—everything seemed unreal, transient, miragelike, and from the very center of my being I recognized the dreamlike nature of it all.

In that moment, I felt the grip of hope and fear relax, the constriction of my ordinary mind loosen into uncontrived, open awareness. I left the monastery filled with a tremendous sense of blessing.

That night at Khanpo Dorje's I had a dream. A huge red horse came thundering up, seven riders on its back. One of the seven grasped my arm and pulled me onto the horse's back, saying, "Now all is well!" and we rode up into the sky.

The next morning my three friends and I made plans to meet in a village across the river and travel together from there. We departed by different roads, having previously left our horses at different landings on the river's south side. Years before, there had been a large boat made of two hollow tree trunks that ferried forty people and a few horses at once, but a drunken brawl during a crossing had sent it swirling downstream. No one had drowned, but the boat was lost and now the banks of the river were dotted with landings for small boats.

On the south side of the river my attendant and I walked up to the house where my horse was stabled. This family had always been very friendly to me, but when they invited me in a sense of unease came over me and I refused, telling them that I would sit in the yard. They brought me a big bottle of *chang;* I drank it and napped for a long time. My attendant woke me up, saying, "Tulku, it's getting late. Either we should stay here overnight or move on now."

"I don't want to stay here. Let's go," I replied. We left— just ahead of Chinese troops who were searching for Khampas, as it turned out—and walked until well after dark. We came to a house of another family I knew well, and without disturbing anyone we turned in for the night. The next morning at about five-thirty I heard a shot. A hundred yards away on the road, the Chinese had shot and killed a monk who was walking to his monastery.

I left early and rode toward the village where I was to meet my three Khampa friends. Suddenly, I heard myself being called. "Tulku! Tulku! Wait!" It was one of the three, a simple fellow, who ran up to me, wheezing with exertion.

"Tulku! You must come! They have arrested the three of us and another man, and they won't let us go unless you vouch for us!"

"What happened?" I asked.

"Last night we decided to camp by the river. After we left you at Khanpo Dorje's, another man joined us and we pitched a tent, bought some *chang* and a big piece of meat and made a fire to roast it. We were just drinking, telling stories and enjoying our food when a Chinese patrol came up and asked us what we were doing. We told them we were only camping until we could ride on the next morning. They said we were lying and accused us of being Khampa thieves. At first we didn't think they were serious because they didn't have any reason to call us thieves, but then they said they were arresting thieves and we would have to come with them.

"We said, 'We're not thieves and if you need someone to back us up, ask Chagdud Tulku. He knows us and he was just with us yesterday. He can tell you who we are.'

"They were willing to accept your word about us, Tulku, but they took the other two to the jail at the military post. They let me go so I could find you and tell you to come to the post and vouch for us."

"You know it won't help!" I exclaimed. "You can't really believe they want me to come to their post only to vouch for you in a case they've trumped up themselves and then they will let all of us free to go our own ways!"

"Oh, yes, Tulku, it will help. You must come so they will release us. Otherwise, who knows what will happen?"

I looked at him hard. It was incredible to me, but I saw that he really did accept the intentions of the Chinese at face value. His foolishness itself convinced me that I would have to go to the post, because if I didn't he would feel as betrayed as a child whose parent refused to protect it from harm.

"If this is what you really want," I said finally, "I'll go to the post. You travel on ahead and I'll make some arrangements here; then I'll follow." The man left cheerfully, and I arranged to have my attendant take my horse home and send messages to my sponsors. My attendant warned me not to go, but I wouldn't listen to him. With a morose good-bye he departed.

I crossed to the north side of the river again, and as I walked up the bank I came upon a boy with three horses. I asked him what he was doing, and he replied, "I am waiting for the Chinese. Yesterday I met some military personnel who ordered me to bring horses to this place today and wait for them."

"They probably aren't coming now. You might as well return home," I suggested. We walked together from the river to the road and down the road a short way. We were trudging along, not talking, when we looked up and saw some military approaching. The boy instantly panicked and bolted into the forest. The Chinese troops, alerted by his suspicious movement, came running up, their guns trained on me.

"Who was that with you?" their leader demanded.

"He is your own helper. He was waiting for you by the river with these horses, and I told him you probably weren't coming, so we walked on together. I don't even know him."

"Who are you?" they asked.

"Chagdud Tulku. I'm walking to your post to vouch for some friends you arrested last night."

"Very good. Now call the boy back."

I shouted into the woods, telling the boy there was nothing to worry about. He climbed out of a tree and turned the horses over to the Chinese. As they mounted I asked them to take my pack of belongings so I wouldn't have to carry them on foot. Taking the pack, they told me to keep walking toward the post and rode off ahead of me. The boy and I continued on, until he turned off toward his own home.

The Chinese post was about ten miles from the river's edge and as always walking was laborious for me. Also it was hot. I walked and rested, walked and rested, and my progress was very slow. As I was sitting by the side of the road, an old man came up to me and asked where I was going. I said, "To the Chinese post."

"You're a Khampa lama, aren't you?"

"Yes."

141

"You know the Chinese are rounding up the Khampas, including the lamas, and throwing them in jail?"

"Yes, I know that."

"Then you know you should be careful. Why don't you hide? Hide today and tonight in a small boat I can take you across the river."

When I explained the situation, he said, "It won't help. All that will happen is that you will be jailed, too, and maybe executed. A lot of Khampa lamas have been executed."

"You are probably right, but there's also a chance they will jail me and let those people go. They are not important to the Chinese. If my life is lost and theirs is spared, then that's enough. Those people requested that I come, so I will."

The old man shook his head, muttering, "It won't help. Really, it won't help." I said good-bye and walked on.

I met a Khampa man coming from the opposite direction. After we had greeted each other, he asked where I was going. I told him the Chinese post. "Don't go there, Lama," he said. "They will put you in jail. There's a band of Khampa resistance fighters nearby and they can conceal you until you can get back across the river." Instinctively I knew he was lying, that there were no Khampa fighters nearby and that he was a Chinese collaborator.

"No. I am going to the post," I told him and walked on.

I stopped at a house and asked to borrow a horse. The people refused my request because the Chinese had warned them that day not to sell anything to a Khampa or to allow a Khampa in their house; if they did, they would receive punishment suitable for a Khampa. "We're sorry but please don't ask us, Lama, because for the safety of our household we can't oblige."

142

I continued walking. When night fell I stopped at another house and asked for shelter. That family, too, had been warned by the Chinese and said they were sorry but they couldn't offer me hospitality. I left, thinking I would lie down alongside the road and sleep, but behind me I heard someone shouting, "Tulku! Tulku! Come back!"

I turned and saw a very old man hobbling along the road.

"Tulku! Please come and stay at my house!" As he came closer I recognized him as someone I had seen participating in the ceremonies I had conducted.

"No," I said. "It could be dangerous for you, because the Chinese will punish you if they learn you have helped a Khampa."

"Tulku, please come. I'm poor and my house isn't much, but if you stay with me, even if the Chinese kill me tomorrow, I will have no regret."

He was so sincere that I accepted his offer. He cleaned his house a bit, put a cloth on a straw cushion to make a special seat and cooked for me. He offered whatever he had with the open generosity of his good heart. At bedtime, however, I decided to sleep on the porch because there were so many fleas.

Sleep didn't come easily, for I knew in continuing to the post I was walking into imprisonment and probable death. But just before the sun rose, I fell asleep and dreamed that a very large man handed me a cup of milk, which I drank. Encouraged by this good sign, I took my leave of the kind old fellow and headed up the road in the cool early morning.

The next person I encountered was a lama from Amdo, a region in the far north, who was the abbot of a Bon monastery nearby. Bon is the ancient, shamanistic religion of Tibet, and despite initial conflict and great philosophical differences, there had been peaceful coexistence between Bon and Buddhist monasteries for centuries.

Again I explained where I was going and why. The abbot tried to dissuade me and offered to hide me in his monastery until a boat could be arranged to take me to the south side of the river. Again I refused and went on my way.

I was very tired—tired from walking the day before, tired from walking this day, tired from a bad night's sleep, tired from repeating my story. I actually found solace in the fact that the Chinese post was only three miles further. I sat down heavily to rest.

A lama who had a startling resemblance to me came up begging alms. He inquired where I was going, and when I repeated my story he said, "Vajra Guru chin chenno"— "Vajra Guru knows." Then he said, "I think today we may die."

I said, "Yes, maybe today."

"You shouldn't go."

"My mind is made up."

"Then be careful."

"You be careful, too," I said, and stood up to go.

Some distance up the road, like a reappearance in a dream, Chinese troops came rushing up and surrounded me. These troops were different from the ones I had encountered the day before, so they demanded to know who I was and where I was going and I explained. They told me to continue on to the post.

About a mile away from my destination, I heard a whistle. I didn't pay attention at first, because the Chinese cars and machines always made strange sounds. Finally I turned around and saw two Tibetan men on horses riding up from behind me. I waited until they caught up to me. "Where are you going?" one of them asked, and I told them the whole story.

"You mustn't go!" one of them exclaimed. "The Chinese detained us last night, and they released us only because they think we will follow their orders and persuade people in the mountain villages to turn in their weapons. If we don't come back in a few days with a stash of guns, they will be hunting us to rearrest us.

"When we were in prison, they asked everyone where you were, and also Kham Wang Tulku and Padlo. They want you and Kham Wang Tulku because of the large ceremonies you led, and Padlo because he is a big man here in Kongpo. They want to cut off any influence you three have, and there is no doubt that they will kill you if you go inside their post. They are devious, murderous liars, and you are giving them satisfaction without helping anyone else if you put yourself in their hands. Don't do it! Come with us!"

When I wouldn't accept their advice, they were almost angry and jerked their horses around to ride off. Then they stopped and one of them said quietly, his eyes filling with tears, "Please, Tulku, don't go. It won't benefit. Please come with us." This time I said yes. Finally the utter futility of the situation released me from it.

I quickly went behind a tree, took my lama's robes off and changed into one of their *chubas*. They gave me a big hat to wear. Then we made some tea as a pretext for their not riding from the post directly. When some Chinese came from the post, the two Tibetans left me by the fire and rode up to them. Both of them had permits. When the Chinese asked about me, they said I was a relative who had come from their village to check up on them. Now that they were released, I would go back straightaway. Seeming to accept this story, the Chinese continued on their way.

Then, unexpectedly, they returned. One of the Tibetans said to me, "Stay here, Tulku. If something made them suspicious and they are going to cause trouble now, we have short knives and we will fight and die to save your life." Again they rode off to meet the Chinese, who merely confirmed something on one of the permits and left.

One of the Tibetans borrowed a horse. We spilled out the tea and rode to an unfrequented spot on the riverbank. I hid alone in the forest near the bank all day, and late that night a friend of the two Tibetan men ferried me across to the south side.

At midnight I knocked on the door of a family I knew to borrow a horse. Without asking any questions they loaned me one. When I reached home, I quickly gathered some food and fled immediately, leaving the horse to be returned by my sponsors.

For the next six months I lived undercover, never staying more than a night or two anywhere, even in remote forests or caves. For a long time the only persons who knew I was alive were the two Tibetans who brought me to the river, the boatman, the family who had loaned me the horse and two other families, one poor and one very prominent, who brought me food in hiding.

Everyone else in Kongpo thought I had been killed by the Chinese because, on the same day that I had met him on the road to the post, the lama who resembled me and was begging alms had been shot by troops. Possibly they had signaled him to come to them and he had run away—the Chinese considered anyone who tried to flee a fair target. Then, seeing his corpse, they thought it was mine. Or possibly they had shot him simply because they mistook him for me. I remembered our conversation about dying that day and I deeply regretted his death.

I had sent a message to Khanpo Dorje asking if I could go to Padma Kod before the passes closed for winter. He sent a message back that I should wait for him. I didn't look forward to months more of hiding, living in one lair after another, but it became an opportunity to practice, to experience the life of the solitary yogi, to stare hard at impermanence and death.

In the early months of 1959 the Khampa military rode into Kongpo and camped in the region of Karma Drolma's family. With the military protection I felt it safe to stay with her in her family's house. It was the first time I had seen her since the marriage arrangements had been made almost a year before. Her father had held to the agreement and by Tibetan custom, which did not depend on legal papers, we were considered married.

We spent ten days together, and they were filled with newfound pleasures. Since I had lived my entire life in the world of monks, lamas and hard-riding Khampas, intimacy with a woman—not only physical, but conversational and in the sharing of daily routines—was a revelation and a delight to me. Karma, twenty years old and eight younger than I, was extremely pretty and had a melodious voice. She also seemed intelligent and quite capable.

Late one night as I was lying in bed waiting for her, my vision opened. I could see the path in the village and two very odd women walking down it. When Karma came into the room, I described what I was seeing to her. "There are two women with baskets on their backs walking through the village."

"What are you talking about? No one goes out at this hour."

"There are two women with baskets on their backs walking through the village, and they are going in the doorway of the house at the bottom of the hill."

She stared at me, perplexed. I went on. "Now they are leaving the house, going down the road, and they have some chopped meat in their baskets." The strange moment of clairvoyance passed and Karma and I went to sleep.

The next morning all the household members were discussing the unexpected death of a woman who lived in the house at the bottom of the hill. Her family said she died for no apparent reason late at night, about the same time we were going to bed. I interpreted my vision to mean that her life had been seized by nonmortals, either the beneficial forces of liberation or the demonic forces of harm.

At the end of this interlude, the Khampa military decided to ride on and camp in a remote site high above the tree line. A monastery associated with my wife's family was located near their camp and I felt I would be fairly safe there. Since Karma was not a fugitive as I was, it seemed easier and safer for her to remain with her family until I received word from Khanpo Dorje about Padma Kod. Regretfully I departed from her and her family. Before I left, Karma gave me an extremely valuable necklace of coral, turquoise and *zi,* stones prized by Tibetans.

She also gave me a precious mold for making clay images of a great treasure discoverer named Gyaltsan Nyingpo. After I arrived at the monastery, I made one thousand such images.

Into the clay I compounded many sacred substances so that the images would be permeated with blessings. The Khampa fighters asked me to do an extensive Vajrakilaya ceremony, and in the course of the three-day ceremony, I gave each soldier one of the Gyaltsan Nyingpo images as a blessing of protection.

On the night before the ceremony I had a vision of my room transforming into a huge prison. I don't know what became of that house, but Kongpo itself became the site of a major concentration camp after the Chinese takeover.

On the second night of the ceremony I had a lucid dream in which I recognized the dream state. I traveled to Guru Rinpoche's pure realm of Zangdog Palri—Glorious Copper-Colored Mountain. Guru Rinpoche looked like a statue on his throne in his celestial palace. Creating through my powers of mind an offering as extensive as the universe, I approached him and told him of the difficulties I was facing. He responded with a prophecy and I awakened greatly reassured.

On the third afternoon, the Vajrakilaya ritual concluded with the placement of sanctified substances in the fire as completely pure offerings to the wisdom beings. The very moment the final offering was made, the fire swirled up violently, sending sparks and smoke back into our faces, and we heard shots in the distance behind us.

There was immediate chaos as the three Khampa generals rallied their troops into a rearguard action and more than a thousand civilians fled for their lives, their yaks, horses and sheep thundering along with them. The Khampa fighters managed to prevent the Chinese from overtaking us, and soon there was a tumultuous river of people and animals moving forward, protected on the flanks and rear by Khampas. The mountainous terrain worked to our advantage, because as the people poured through the narrow gorges, the Khampas ambushed the Chinese who tried to follow.

Unbelievably, it was in the midst of this pell-mell flight that I met Khanpo Dorje again, along with his brother and his nephew. I was overjoyed to see him, but I knew we were not going to Padma Kod now. We were going to India.

9

Flight

OUR ESCAPE from Tibet consisted of a series of fortunate events and mishaps spanned by unrelieved, grinding endurance. My teacher and his brother were both elderly men, I was a poor walker and Khanpo Dorje's nephew was a headstrong young man with a good heart but unreliable judgment. This nephew, in fact, caused our first mischance.

After the Vajrakilaya ceremony concluded with a full-fledged flight from the Chinese, the mass of Tibetans were headed toward the monastery of Sang-ngag Chhöling across the Dagpo pass, protected by the rearguard action of the Khampa military. On the way we came to a place where the trail branched. The four of us stopped to do divinations, which were very good for splitting off from the group and going separately on this secondary route. However, Khanpo Dorje's nephew strongly opposed this plan.

"How could it be safer to go without the military!" he exclaimed. "We will be unprotected in a long valley with the Chinese at our backs."

Khanpo Dorje replied that the divinations had been very good.

151

"Many lamas do divinations these days and many lamas have been killed," the nephew countered stubbornly.

His father quickly reprimanded him. "Don't talk that way! Khanpo Dorje is a great lama and he is the elder among us. You are not in a position to question the wisdom of his choice."

The nephew refused to give up because he was convinced his father and his uncle would be killed if they left the protection of the military. Tears in his eyes, he pleaded, "Please don't make this decision."

Finally, Khanpo Dorje conceded, saying, "If you insist and will be miserable otherwise, we will follow the military." Later we would learn that those who escaped by the secondary route through the valley were able to keep their possessions intact and to walk directly toward the protection of the Indian army across the Himalayas. We, however, had to begin discarding things immediately and fled by a dangerous, circuitous route that would delay our reaching India for months.

We traveled on horseback without stopping for four days and reached the Dagpo pass in the dark hours of predawn on the fifth. With no tea, no food and no sleep, strange images floated into my field of vision. The path across the pass was firm, but on either side stood deep snow. We would move forward a short distance, then everyone—a thousand people and hundreds of animals—would halt because a person or a pack animal had tumbled into the snow. Regrouping on the other side of the mountain, we pushed forward to the monastery of Sang-ngag Chhöling at dawn.

For days we had held Sang-ngag Chhöling as our destination, a place where we could stop at last. But suddenly the Khampa military sounded an alarm, saying the Chinese were forging toward the Dagpo pass and urging us to continue our flight immediately. We heeded this advice and fled, but at least half the people were too exhausted to go on until they at least had eaten something. Five hundred were captured and taken back by the Chinese. This news, relayed by the Khampas, was deeply depressing to the rest of us.

We were fleeing toward a second pass called the Lungjug, a pass so narrow and treacherous that the horses could not go across. Most of the belongings we had not already jettisoned we discarded now, carrying only the most precious, sacred objects on our backs. It was while crossing this pass that I came to the melancholy realization that this was the end of my life as I had known it. My possessions, my relatives, my monastery, my country—layer by layer these had been stripped away. I was dazed by sleeplessness, hunger and loss. I felt as if I had entered the *bardo,* the intermediate state between death and rebirth where one experiences existence as completely insubstantial and miragelike. Like a wayfarer in the *bardo,* I knew that this journey would end only in an inconceivably different existence.

On the south side of the Lungjug pass we entered the region Tibetans call "land of wild men" and Indians call "land of *nagas.*" Nagaland is the northeast region of India, adjacent to Burma. Its borders remained largely undefined by the governments of India and Tibet but would become hotly disputed between India and China. With its extensive tropical rainforests, it was inhabited by primitives who hunted with poison arrows and believed it was virtuous to kill and to make animal sacrifices. If an important family member died, they would decapitate hundreds of animals and put their heads on stakes around the grave. We were very gloomy while in this hot, savage land.

We came to a mountain named Saru, sacred to the

Vajrayana Buddhist deity Chakrasamvara. We decided to remain in the mountain highlands for a time because we were certain to die in the blazing heat of the Indian plain. A Bhutanese man joined our group, and another lama with four companions was camped on the mountain. We all lived on cornmeal, sold to us for the exorbitant price of one silver coin per cup, and a garliclike plant. Neither the cornmeal nor the vegetable seemed very appetizing to a Tibetan. Then someone in the other lama's group shot a yak and shared the meat with us. This gave us strength at a time when we were extremely weak.

After three months at Saru, dream signs and divinations indicated a bad turn in our situation and we knew we should move deeper into India. Saru stood in the vaguely delineated border area of Nagaland so we definitely were not out of the reach of the Chinese. We had to cross two mountains to reach an encampment of the Indian army, and we sent a man ahead to try to find help. I was very concerned that Khanpo Dorje and his brother might not be able to walk the distance.

The other group left with us, but as we set out three of them began to express doubts—they would probably die in India of heat or starvation; maybe the Chinese would not be so bad in Tibet; certainly it would be better to die in Tibet than in India.

The three went on in this way, delaying us as they fell into endless discussion, until I noticed some men coming across the ridge of the mountain, possibly a Chinese patrol. There was no time to waste if Khanpo Dorje and his brother were going to make it out, but at that moment one of the three announced, "I'm not going with you. I'm turning back to surrender myself." The other two said they were going back with him. I looked hard at them and knew full well that their courage was not of the caliber to withstand Chinese interrogation. They would betray us, and Khanpo Dorje and everyone else, including them, would be killed. Suddenly I became furious.

Yanking a small pistol from my belt, I aimed it at them. "That won't work. You have no choice now to surrender to the Chinese. Your choice is to go forward or die where you stand." My voice was steady but my face twitched.

Time seemed to halt in an instant of intense clarity. No one spoke or moved, until one of the three said, "Right, Tulku. We're going with you and the others." It was as if a spell had been broken. Immediately everyone was all haste and efficiency.

Khanpo Dorje and the others went forward while I stayed behind with two men to intercept the intruders and guard our rear if necessary. The intruders, however, turned out to be the man we had sent ahead to the army encampment and the porters he had returned with. With their assistance we were able to trek through the forest swiftly, which was fortunate, for the next day our camp at Saru was overrun by Chinese troops and we had to dodge airplanes so as not to be strafed from the air.

Finally, after crossing the mountains, we saw the Indian army encampment. We were still in an area of Nagaland that Tibetans called Tibet, although the Indians stationed troops there without challenge. Their camp was in a valley surrounded by high mountains, in a climate that alternated between drenching monsoon summers and deep-snow winters. The climate, the mountains and the inaccessibility by road—supplies were air-dropped—created a sense of isolation. There seemed to be no expectation that this isolation would be violated by attack. Command was lax, military preparedness low.

Near the camp our groups separated. The other lama immediately reported to the Indian army so that he and his friends could receive food. Their supplies had dwindled and they were quite hungry. The lama soon made himself useful to the army command by his skill at stopping monsoon rains. Skeptical at first, the officers became convinced of his extraordinary abilities after the lama had a number of successes at keeping the skies clear on exactly the days when there were to be air drops. They eventually asked him to stay and offered to pay him for his weather work. He declined this offer and left before we did.

Our group still had some food supplies and it was just about harvesttime, so we decided to take residence in a cave overlooking both camp and valley until we could purchase new supplies from local farmers. The military knew we were there, and with our prayers and ceremonies we supported the other lama's efforts to stop rain.

During this time I had various dreams of shaking dirt out of my clothes. According to Tibetan dream signs this meant I was going to lose money—the opposite, contact with filth and excrement, being the dream sign of wealth. I did prayers and practice in the hope that the signs would change, but they did not.

Other dream signs were not good either, nor was the outer situation. As more Tibetan refugees gathered in the vicinity of the camp, they began to warn the Indian command about the strength and discipline of the Chinese army and to encourage a military alert. The command was very self-confident and some of the officers quite pompous. They were not receptive to strategic advice from ragged Tibetans who had just lost their country.

Despite all of this, we stayed on. The other lama had left, Khanpo Dorje urged many Tibetan refugees to continue their flight, yet we ourselves did not leave until one day when we knew intuitively that danger was imminent. That day we packed up our remaining possessions and took them down to the village, where we arranged for them to be held overnight. Then we returned to the cave to sleep, planning to leave at daylight the next morning.

In the predawn, at about three o'clock, the valley exploded with the fire of heavy artillery and automatic weapons. During the night the Chinese forces had positioned themselves so effectively that they had captured the village and sent the Indian troops in a disorderly flight from the encampment before any defense could be mounted. Their objective was apparently limited to military control over the Tibetan population and the valley, and did not extend to annihilation of the enemy. Had they chosen to, the Chinese could have killed the Indian troops almost to a man. They were restrained by the official policy between India and China at that time— "Panch Steel," mutual coexistence. It would be violated by China several years later, but for much larger stakes than that isolated valley and a few refugees.

In our cave high above the valley we still had a chance to join the retreating Indian army and escape, but the possessions we had left in the village were irretrievable. I lost five hundred silver coins and had only fifty left; Khanpo Dorje lost his last and most sacred statues and relics. There was no time to mourn, however. We gathered our bedding and fled through the forest toward the Indian troops.

The main trail out of the valley led across a bridge. From a distance we could see that the Chinese troops had already taken it, so staying under cover, we headed downstream. Passage was very difficult and often we could do no more than crawl along the steep, rocky mountainsides, clinging to roots and vines. In my heart I wondered if I could lead my elderly teacher and his elderly brother to safety, especially now that we could not follow the main trail and were away from the protection of the Indian troops.

That night we bivouacked in thick undergrowth. As troubled as my mind was, I slept soundly until I was awakened by shots. Not twenty feet away, Chinese troops were firing at the Indians. After a while, without detecting us, they moved on, as did we.

We traveled through the forest for three days, afraid that the Chinese might be in pursuit along the main trail. We were famished, and progress was so difficult that we did not cover more than two miles during that time. Then Khanpo Dorje's nephew fell and seriously injured his leg. We had to hide and rest for three more days, but we were able to obtain some rice from Indian soldiers. That plain, boiled rice, without salt or butter, tasted as delicious as anything I've ever eaten.

After the nephew recovered enough to hobble along with the help of a stick, we set out again along the river. Swollen from the monsoon rains, it churned muddy water and boulders as it coursed through the narrow mountain gorge. The trail switched from bank to bank, and we had to cross the river thirteen times, clinging to bridges fabricated of woven vines. Most of these bridges had no planks, and it was dizzying to look down through the gaping mesh at the swirling turbulence below. We had a Bhutanese companion, familiar with such bridges in his own country, who stepped across quickly, lightly. We Tibetans crossed ponderously, almost

Sechhen Kongtrul

Mountains of Tromt'har

Tenp'hel Gonpa

Barley fields, Nyagrong

Houses and drying barley, Nyagrong

Chagdud Gonpa

Women dancing, Nyagrong

Khanpo Dorje

Chagdud Tulku, shortly
after his escape to India;
ca. 1961

H. H. Dilgo Khyentse Rinpoche (right)
with Trungpa Rinpoche

H. H. Dudjom Rinpoche as a young man

Lamas gathered for the Nyingma *kama* transmission. H. H. Dudjom Rinpoche, seated, center. Standing: Chagdud Tulku, left; Mindroling Trichhen Rinpoche, third from left; Khanpo Dorje, eighth from left; Trulzhig Rinpoche, fifth from right; Tingboche Tulku, third from right. Kalimpong, India, 1961

(Left) Karma Drolma, Chagdud Tulku's first wife, Bir; (right) Chagdud Tulku, Bir; (bottom) Chagdud Tulku and friends, Bir

Karma Drolma with
children Dawa Lhamo
and Jigmed Norbu, Bir

Jigmed Norbu, Tibet, 1987

Chagdud Tulku on his way to receive empowerments from H.H. Khyentse Rinpoche, Bir

Women prostrating in doorway of monastery in Tso Pema

Majnukatilla, the Tibetan refugee camp in Delhi

Chagdud Tulku in procession, Boudhanath, Nepal

(Left) H. H. Khyentse Rinpoche; (right) H. H. Khyentse Rinpoche's last teaching to Chagdud Tulku, France, 1990; (bottom) Chagdud Tulku, Boudhanath, Nepal, 1978

Chagdud Tulku and Jane, wedding day, South
Lake Tahoe, California, 1979

Jane, 1986

Chagdud Tulku, in procession to Tenp'hel Gonpa, 1987

T'hrinlay Wangmo, Chagdud Tulku's sister, 1987

Chagdud Tulku with Tulku Jigmed Namgyal, Tromt'har, 1987

Tulku Jigmed Namgyal, his son T'hrinlay Odzer and his daughter Kunlu, 1987

Procession to Chagdud Gonpa, 1987

Chagdud Gonpa

Anjang Rinpoche, Chagdud Tulku, Tulku Ado, Gyurmed Dorje Rinpoche,
at Chagdud Gonpa, 1987

Chagdud Gonpa monks, 1987

(Top) Chagdud Tulku giving
blessings, 1987; (bottom) the oldest
Chagdud Gonpa monk, who
witnessed Tanpai Gyaltsan
give Dawa Drolma the reliquary

(Top) Tulku Arig a few
months before his death,
1987; (bottom) the
infant incarnation of
Tulku Arig, 1991

Some of Chagdud Tulku's Western Students, Oregon, 1987

paralyzed with fear, and our heavy, unbalanced tread set the bridge swinging in a wide arc above the wild water.

The trail along the almost vertical bank was often no more than an extremely narrow ledge. We would flatten ourselves against the bank, extend one foot forward, then draw the second up behind it, clutching at wickerlike roots for support. I was moving along such a ledge when I came to a gap in the wicker and had to grasp a shrub to steady myself. Suddenly its roots gave way.

I toppled backward into the river thirty feet below, where I was dragged under instantly by my heavy pack. In the roar of the current I could hear the rocks tumbling along the riverbed. My mind became very clear, and the first thoughts that arose were "I'm not dead. There's no pain." Like most Tibetans, I don't know how to swim, but I began to thrash until my hand found something solid. I grabbed it and was able to pull my head above water. The object was the branch of a huge tropical tree that had fallen into the river and formed an eddy. Because of it I hadn't been swept downstream and now I clung to it, completely spent and gasping for breath. Khanpo Dorje's nephew was the first to reach me, and he helped me out. My pack, loaded with cushions and bedding, seemed as heavy as stone. We left it by the river, and walked until we found a cave. The Bhutanese went back for the pack and we made a huge fire to dry our gear.

The trauma of falling into the river drained me of strength and confidence. The bridges, ledges and mountain trails, the leeches that constantly plagued us, the lack of food, the uncertainty about Chinese pursuit, the inability, since the nephew had hurt his leg, of four out of five of us to walk well—everything now seemed overwhelmingly difficult and daunting to me.

159

It was just in this time of need that Dorje, our Bhutanese companion, demonstrated completely selfless service. When we came to treacherous passages, he would carry our gear, making trip after trip. Then he would assist Khanpo Dorje and his brother, one at a time. When we stopped, he would gather bamboo shoots and other edible plants he was familiar with, the environment and vegetation of Nagaland being similar to Bhutan's. These vegetables sustained us for some days. With his agility, his skills and his good heart, he was crucial to our survival during this time.

Khanpo Dorje himself was calm and uncomplaining, practical about arrangements, but unwavering in his recognition of the absolute nature of reality, beyond the mere play of phenomenal events. He transmitted the profound meaning of dharma during this time as powerfully as before, though without formal discourses. Throughout our flight I never lost sight of the privilege of being with him, of my unsurpassed good fortune amid apparent bad circumstances.

About twelve days after we had fled the Chinese attack on the Indian army encampment, the worst of our trek was over. We were able to join Indian troops going in our direction, and they gave us rice, lentils, coconut oil and salt. We were definitely out of the reach of the Chinese so we stopped for several days to rest. Then we set out for the final, much easier leg of our journey, which took one more week.

We finally arrived at the army post at Lemigang. As Tibetans poured in, the Indians processed identification papers and moved everyone along as quickly as possible so that the post would not become a flashpoint for hostilities with the Chinese. I had heard rumors that in India if you were a male between six and eighteen you were sent to school, between eighteen and twenty-nine you were inducted into the military, between thirty and sixty you were sent to work on a farm and older than sixty you were sent to an old-age home. I was twenty-nine, but claimed to be thirty-four. I was quite clear about not wanting to be drafted into the Indian military, but falsifying my record turned out to be unnecessary, since the rumor was not true.

Khanpo Dorje, his brother and I, all obviously unable to walk further, were helicoptered from Lemigang to the next refugee intake center, a place called Dagpo Ricchog. Khanpo Dorje's nephew and the Bhutanese Dorje walked another week to meet us there. We stayed in this center for one month and then were flown to Missamari, a large Tibetan refugee camp in Assam.

The night before we flew to Missamari I had a dream that I was taking an airplane to an unknown destination. In the dream I asked where I was flying, and someone replied, "America." When I awakened the next morning, I asked some people where America was. Most didn't know, but finally someone said, "It's very far away and it's a land of blue-eyed demons."

That day we flew in an old propeller plane to Assam. The ride was very rough, and one time, as the plane plunged in an air pocket, I thought my mind itself had moved. At the camp at Missamari we joined thousands of other Tibetan refugees, all in transit to a new life in exile.

10

In Exile

MISSAMARI was located by a river on a sandy flat that had been pockmarked by bombing during World War II. To accommodate the influx of refugees, the Indian government had thrown up rows of bamboo barracks that housed sixty people each. There was no sanitation and the water was contaminated. Amoebic dysentery spread through the camp, and Tibetans, exhausted, starving, heartsick and stunned by the blazing heat, died by the hundreds. The cremation fires adjacent to the camps burned constantly, fueled by fifteen or twenty bodies daily. In the pall cast by sickness and death, the survivors talked endlessly of returning to their homeland or helplessly of where they might be sent in India.

The Indian government provided the camp rations of rice, lentils, meat several times a week, dried milk, cheese and tomatoes. Most of us did not know what to do with the tomatoes, and red, rotten heaps of them sprung up around the camp. Nor did we, as mountain people from a relatively germ-free environment, know how to cope with the scorching temperature and the diseases we encountered. I went around with a thick blanket wrapped about my abdomen because someone had advised me that I must wrap up or the heat would make me sick. I was sick anyway, and one day, while I was lying down near Khanpo Dorje, I began hallucinating. I asked, "Are you doing mirror *puja*? I am seeing things."

He murmured, "No, no. I'm not doing anything." The next thing I remember, I woke up in the hospital. From then on, for the remainder of my eight-month stay at Missamari, I was in and out of the hospital until the doctors decided that since I was terminally ill, a hospital bed was wasted on me and I should go back to the barracks. The doctors weren't heartless, but with so many critically ill patients, they had to make such decisions.

One day a cleaning lady from the hospital came to see how I was and recommended I take parasite medicine. Although I told her the doctors had given me parasite medicine many times before, she said, "Never mind. I am going to bring you medicine." The next day she came back with some little white pills marked with clovers that she had filched from the hospital, saying, "I think these are the pills for parasites. Take four now and two later, and see what happens." When she left I took three pills.

That night I slept well and in the morning I was hungry. I told a friend to bring some *tsampa* made of roasted wheat, and after I had finished one ball of dough, I wanted another. My friend hesitated. "Do you really want to eat so much after weeks of eating almost nothing at all?" I did, and after eating I felt fine.

My practice was greatly reduced during this illness, and I had focused on reciting a hundred thousand prayers to be reborn in Guru Rinpoche's pureland and offering seven butterlamps daily, using my uneaten ration of coconut oil. After this turning point, on Losar, the Tibetan New Year's Day, I decided to concentrate on longevity practice to hasten my recovery. That same day a man came to our barracks who had planned to do longevity practice himself but was suddenly called on to resettle to another camp. He offered me the *torma,* a symbolic offering sculpted of dough or clay, that he had prepared for his practice. I was extremely pleased to receive it for I felt it was a good sign. Within a week of beginning this practice I was able to get out of bed and, with the help of friends and a cane, to walk outside. At that moment a light rain began to fall and it felt like medicine as it touched my skin.

Khanpo Dorje, his brother and his nephew had left Missamari sometime before, relocating to Kalimpong, a town in the mountains of West Bengal on the border of India and Tibet. Kalimpong had long been a trading center for Indians and Tibetans, and some Tibetans had established residence there generations before the conflict with the Chinese, making it easier for refugees to settle in that locality.

Khanpo Dorje had received an invitation from a sponsor in Kalimpong and had invited me to accompany him. I declined, primarily because I had no money and would have to accept his support, which I did not think was proper, but also because I wanted to wait for my wife Karma.

After his departure, while I was still very ill, I learned that Karma had arrived in India and that she was with another man. This didn't disturb me because it was natural that Karma, thinking I had probably died, should turn to and rely on someone else. However, I felt honor bound to return her gift of a valuable necklace with many large pieces of turquoise, coral and *zi.*

When I was well enough, I received redistribution papers to go to a camp two hours away from Missamari. I made arrangements to meet Karma there. Our meeting was calm, with many long silences, and finally she told me that she was very happy to find me alive and wished that our relationship would be that of man and wife. I was glad to reestablish this relationship. Although we never married officially, in the social turmoil of that time such legalities were of little consequence. Together we went to visit her mother and other relatives, who were stationed in a camp six hours away. The night before we arrived, they suffered a tremendous loss when a thief stole all the wealth they had carried out of Tibet.

The night after we arrived I had a vivid dream of a huge tiger surrounded by flames, stalking in the sky. It approached, paused directly above me and withdrew, disappearing into light. Upon awaking I knew it wasn't a good sign, and later, after we had relocated in Kalimpong, the Chinese army made a fierce attack on the camp, pouncing across the border like a tiger. Though none of our relatives were killed, other Tibetans were.

While still in this camp I relapsed into illness, as debilitating as before. Then one night I dreamed that a woman put two pills in my mouth. I woke up still tasting the pills and soon I recovered my health. From that time on I was able to turn my attention to helping others who were sick and dying, yet my personal troubles were not over. Karma had given birth to our child, a son who by all signs and predictions was a great *tulku,* the incarnation of Garzhe Khanpo. One night, a week after his birth, the baby began to cry and could not be comforted. In the morning he died.

Everyone wept except me. I was very sad that the world had lost the benefit of the rebirth of Garzhe Khanpo and also to see the suffering of my wife, but somehow my grief could not be released by tears. There were so many deaths, so many great lamas lost, so many family tragedies—within a short time there would be three more deaths in our own family including that of Karma's mother—that the causes for tears, and equally for compassion, were limitless.

In the relocation camp people sometimes made offerings to me when I did prayers and rituals, and this support was very helpful. I had arrived in Missamari with almost no money and had spent that on two silver offering bowls and some cloth for a robe. The robe I had worn from Tibet had been quite fine in its day, silk padded with cotton, but by the time I reached India the silk was tattered and ornamented with strange cotton blossoms where the batting had popped through. Eventually I accumulated two hundred Indian rupees—about twenty-five dollars—and I considered myself quite prosperous.

One ceremony I felt honored to conduct during those months in the camps was *p'howa* for the old man who had offered me food and shelter in Kongpo when everyone else had turned me away for fear of Chinese retaliation. My prayer was that his kindness to me and whatever other merit he had accumulated would ripen into a blissful rebirth in the pureland of Amitabha Buddha and that he would find ultimate liberation.

News came that His Holiness Dudjom Rinpoche would be giving the empowerments of the Rinchhen Terdzod and of the Nyingma *kama*, the lineage of direct spoken teachings passed down from teacher to student over the generations. The empowerments would take place in Kalimpong, two days' train ride away, and Karma and I decided to go.

We traveled with an old lama and two monks. The two

monks did not pay the fare, and throughout the trip they ducked the conductors successfully because the trains were extremely crowded. We reached Siliguri and traveled to Darjeeling and Kalimpong by bus. The road was spectacular, running along a high ridge with the Himalayas to the north and dropping to the plains of India to the south. Kalimpong itself was high, cool and pleasant. His Holiness Dudjom Rinpoche had a residence there, which made it an auspicious place to settle. His Holiness Karmapa, the supreme head of the Kagyu lineage, had requested relief funds to be designated for refugees in Kalimpong, and the Indian government agreed, ensuring that we would at least have food to eat.

Khanpo Dorje was in Kalimpong, and I had an opportunity to visit with him for two days, which turned out to be the last time I ever saw him alive. Shortly after, he moved to Darjeeling and then to Bhutan, where he was revered. He died several years later while I was in a refugee camp in Orissa, but because Orissa is a remote area of India, I did not learn of his death for three months. I was grief-stricken when I heard the news, and in that moment I saw him one last time, in a vision so vivid it was as though he were actually present.

In Kalimpong we set up a small tent and the five of us settled in. Karma and I attended the empowerments every day, as did the two monks. The old lama, who had already received these empowerments, stayed behind to guard our possessions, particularly a bag the monks owned and were extremely concerned about.

The monks went around the camp begging each day, and when they did not collect enough from the other refugees, they would come back to the tent bemoaning their slim fare. We would then share what we had with them, but after a while Karma and the old lama began to think it was odd that though these monks supposedly had nothing, they guarded their bag with such concern. One day while the monks were out begging, curiosity overcame Karma and the lama. They opened the bag, peered inside and saw eight essences of musk deer, worth a fortune in India, and three hundred silver coins. We didn't confront them about their deceit, but we no longer shared our food with them.

At times I was thoroughly disillusioned by the conduct of my fellow refugees, and I especially regretted that one of the worst aspects of Tibet, sectarian politics among the various traditions of Tibetan Buddhism, had not been completely abandoned on the other side of the Himalayas. The Dalai Lama and four heads of the major traditions—the Gandan Tri Rinpoche for the Gelugpa, Sakya Trizin for the Sakyapa, the Karmapa for the Kagyupa and Dudjom Rinpoche for the Nyingmapa—were exemplary, cooperative with one another, working to benefit all Tibetans impartially and at the same time working to preserve their own traditions.

Tibetan intermediaries at a lower level, however, often favored the members of their own tradition, particularly with regard to assigning camps and countries for resettlement. This added unnecessarily to the anxiety and despair of Tibetans at a time when they were already under great stress. Then, as individuals, some refugees like the two monks behaved in callous and unethical ways, though many others conducted themselves with great forbearance in the face of their difficulties, compromising neither faith nor ethics in adapting to their new environment.

In Kalimpong the Nyingmapas decided as a group that they needed a spokesperson to present their issues to Dudjom Rinpoche and to convey his wishes and guidance to them. There was one particularly devoted student of Dudjom

Rinpoche named Gyurmed, and the consensus was that no one could represent the Nyingmas better. His Holiness was pleased with this choice.

Gyurmed himself, however, was utterly dismayed. Not once had he ever brought unhappiness to the mind of his lama. He had served him perfectly as a practitioner and created no friction by dealing with ordinary issues. Now, as the chosen purveyor of the group's ordinary day-to-day business, he was sure conflict would arise and mar his relationship with Dudjom Rinpoche. In his anxiety he couldn't sleep. He went to Dudjom Rinpoche and begged to be released from this duty. "I am not capable of filling this position without offending everyone and bringing shame to you as a teacher. Please don't require it of me."

Dudjom Rinpoche was sympathetic to Gyurmed's distress and did not insist. Then he called me and asked me to serve as the liaison. I agreed to the task with an untroubled mind, viewing it as an opportunity to help implement His Holiness's activity. We began work on a complex to house monks, nuns and lay people. It was only a bamboo frame with a canvas roof, but it was adequate for our needs and we felt quite fortunate. I worked hard on this building project for some months, supervising and helping with the construction.

During our stay in Kalimpong, His Holiness Khyentse Rinpoche, whom I had first met at Dzongsar Monastery in Eastern Tibet, also gave a number of empowerments, which I attended. Our relationship as lama and disciple deepened from that time onward. His kindness to me would be immeasurable in years to come, and on several occasions the power of his blessings would sustain me in the face of life-threatening obstacles.

My dreams turned very bad again, indicating that the

Chinese might attack across the border. When they actually did attack the camp where I had had my stalking-tiger dream, intense anxiety rippled through Kalimpong. We dared not sleep soundly at night.

His Holiness Dudjom Rinpoche decided to travel by plane and car to Tso Pema, a sacred site in the foothills of the western Indian Himalayas, to give oral instructions for certain Nyingma practices. About sixty persons decided to go along, traveling by train and bus. Karma and I packed with no intention of returning to the constant anxiety of living so near the Chinese military. It was relatively easy to resettle because we had only two or three suitcases of belongings.

Getting on the train, however, became a nightmare because there were so many of us and the railroad car was already extremely crowded. There was a great deal of calling back and forth, shoving and passing baggage through the windows. In the press of the crowd one man had his reliquary, with his money and sacred objects, cut from a cord around his body. He was a big man and courageous, but pinned in the throng, he found himself helpless. Once on the train, we saw that he was bleeding from a wound inflicted by the thief's knife.

There were no seats, of course, and we faced days and nights of standing, leaning against our luggage, one of us wounded, and Gyurmed, Dudjom Rinpoche's best student, now quite sick. An Indian fellow suggested we transfer to an empty car. We couldn't believe our good luck—and we shouldn't have. Two hours later the car was disconnected from the main train and we were left stranded. When it was clear we were not going anywhere, we climbed down and were confronted by Indian train officials who demanded to see our tickets. Almost no one had a ticket because most of us were destitute and usually the tickets were not even checked. Then they asked for our passports, all of which had expired. The officials confiscated these, took us to a nearby building and gave us some food and firewood. Three days later they returned with the passports updated and sent us on our way. The Indian authorities were often that way, easy and accommodating, sympathetic to us as poverty-stricken refugees.

Our delays were not over, however, because at the next major train station we had to get off to take care of Gyurmed, whose health was failing at an alarming rate. We went to a *dharamsala,* a rest house built for travelers that cost only one rupee a night. The next morning Gyurmed's wife summoned me. I found him before an open book, a commentary on the signs of dying for a practitioner of the Great Perfection. Then he passed away, his eyes slightly open, in a relaxed attitude of meditation.

We did not notify the Indian authorities, because we knew they would insist on cremating him straightaway. According to our custom, it was necessary to leave the body untouched for at least twenty-four hours, preferably three days. We decided to summon the authorities the next morning, and when they arrived they were very perturbed. Why had we waited to call them? Why had we traveled with someone so ill in the first place? When they had thoroughly chastised us, they brought wood for Gyurmed's cremation, and after the ceremony, they sent us on our way.

We were very happy to arrive at Tso Pema at last. It is where, in the eighth century, Padmasambhava meditated with his wisdom consort, the Indian princess Mandarava. The king of the region, who was the father of Mandarava, became furious with Padmasambhava and commanded that he be seized and burned alive. When the king's emissaries returned to the pyre to inspect the charred remains, they found Padmasambhava meditating on a magnificent lotus above a miraculously formed lake. Tso (lake) Pema (lotus) became the name of the site.

When we arrived, we found a small village and monastery beside the lake and a community of Tibetan yogis living in caves on the mountainside above, where the original caves of Padmasambhava and Mandarava are located. Dudjom Rinpoche's teachings were given in a small Nyingma monastery beside the lake, a peaceful and inspiring place.

During this time my dreams vacillated between terrible omens and signs of great spiritual blessing. I dreamed that I was trapped in the hollow of a stone animal's horn, embedded in the earth and so tightly squeezed I couldn't get out, that I suffered amid raging storms with lightning and hail and that my house was covered with a thick, black yak-felt cloth. Each of these dreams indicated that powerful negative energies were overtaking my life, and to avert them I arranged for ceremonies and recited strong prayers for protection. The dreams soon abated.

Perhaps I was not the only one with forebodings of difficulties. At the conclusion of his dharma instruction, a few days before his return flight to Kalimpong, His Holiness Dudjom Rinpoche summoned a seer to determine whether there would be obstacles during the return trip.

The seer said, "This is very strange. I see a beautiful Padmasambhava statue encaged in an iron fence with iron thorns."

Everyone agreed that this was bad sign and the seer was asked again about the trip. "I see the dharma protector Lijin

Harleg coming forth with a short, strong black man with many eyes on his arms—the protector Rahula—and the protector Shanpa in the form of a red man. These three dharma protectors are going into the fence and bringing out the Padmasambhava statue."

At this, His Holiness dismissed further inquiry and shrugged off concern. "The outcome is good, so we need not worry," he said. Yet when his plane landed at Siliguri, the airfield nearest Kalimpong, the police were waiting to arrest him on trumped-up charges. The Tibetans in his entourage and those who had come to the airport were unable to dissuade them, apparently because it had been a Tibetan in an influential position who, out of malice or some other extreme distortion of mind, had made the allegations against His Holiness.

When the news broke, a tremor went through the whole refugee community. It was beyond belief that our revered lama, the supreme head of the Nyingmapa, Padmasambhava's representative on earth, could be thrown in jail. And if he could be jailed on an unsubstantiated and capricious charge, who could be safe? Everyone started writing letters and sending telegrams. Some went directly to His Holiness the Dalai Lama, who responded effectively and without hesitation by calling Nehru, the Indian prime minister. He told Nehru that there had been a grave mistake and asked him to intervene. His Holiness Dudjom Rinpoche was released immediately, having been in jail for three days.

We felt great relief, and extreme gratitude to the Dalai Lama, when this episode was over. However, we could not entirely erase the memory of one or more Tibetans having wronged such a high, pure lama, or the fear that it might happen again.

THE SIXTY PEOPLE who had traveled together from Kalimpong to Tso Pema dispersed after Dudjom Rinpoche's release. Some went to work on the roads in northern India, some begged alms, some engaged in trade. I had caught a skin disease, probably ringworm, that completely exasperated me by its itchiness. Hoping it could be healed, I went into retreat in a deep, gloomy cave for several weeks. I had only *tsampa* and tea and a small piece of candle so I could read my text. Mostly I sat in the dark, barely able to see my teacup even during the day. I did extensive mantra recitation.

A Tibetan man had offered to serve me, to keep the tea replenished and to bring me a bowl of *tsampa* three times a day. One day the *tsampa* tasted raw and terrible. I couldn't talk and break my chain of mantra recitation, so I gesticulated and scowled. My attendant took the bowl out into the sunlight and I heard him swear fiercely. He came back in the cave and explained apologetically that he had dipped into a bag of wheat flour by mistake. We had a good laugh, though I was fortunate to have been spared an intense stomachache.

Toward the end of my retreat I dreamed that a woman came and pointed to an ugly red insect with hundreds of legs that was scurrying by. "Quick!" she ordered. "Encircle that insect with fiery embers!" Without hesitation I did so, and the ring of embers slowly contracted until the insect burned to an ash and disappeared. After that my skin problem also disappeared.

Upon completing this retreat I went down the mountain to the lakeside village. Many refugees were still hoping to resettle in Padma Kod on the Indian side of the border. At His Holiness Dudjom Rinpoche's request I collected names and passport numbers, and he turned these over to the Indian government to process. Ultimately Padma Kod was denied as a resettlement region, probably because the Indian government feared it would have to fend off constant Chinese attacks across the border.

Again I returned to retreat, this time served by a young monk named Dawa Chhödrag. One of his functions was to go down the mountain to collect the mail, because letters often arrived from His Holiness Dudjom Rinpoche keeping me informed of events involving the Nyingmas. Then one night I dreamed that I was riding a black horse, trying to ford a river, and had to turn back. I understood from the dream that my retreat would be interrupted, and indeed a request came from His Holiness to collect the names and passport information of two hundred Nyingma Tibetans who would be willing to resettle in Switzerland. I did this, traveling to many camps to compile the list, and everyone was organized to go. Eventually, however, this plan, too, fell through. Disappointments were common in those days.

I returned to Tso Pema, and now my dreams were splendid and full of promise that I would receive a practice by which I could benefit many people. This came about when I met a monk who held the Red Tara cycle of Orgyan T'hrinlay Lingpa, the great Apong Terton. Apong Terton had been a renowned Nyingma lama and was the treasure discoverer of a profound Tara cycle. On his deathbed he instructed a monk whom he had fully endowed with the blessings of the Tara practice by empowerment and instruction to come to him in his next incarnation when he was seventeen years of age and to reempower him into his treasure. The monk promised to do so.

As it happened, however, the Chinese invaded Tibet and the monk was forced to flee to Bhutan. Apong Terton was reborn as Sakya Trizin, supreme head of the Sakyapa tra-

175

dition, and lived as a refugee in a monastery in Dehra Dun in northern India. As His Holiness Sakya Trizin approached the age of seventeen, the monk tried desperately to travel to Dehra Dun, but could not obtain permission from the Indian government. Six years lapsed before the monk reached his former lama and had an audience with him. To their surprise, Sakya Trizin's monks were dismissed and His Holiness prepared to take an empowerment from this rather humble-looking visiting monk. Sakya Trizin received initiation into the entire Red Tara cycle at this time.

Now this monk was in Tso Pema, and he offered to give me the empowerment. I was extremely pleased. Although I had done extensive Tara practice and extensive practice of other red deities of the Padma (Lotus) family, I had never received a Red Tara practice. I knew that this was the auspicious fulfillment of my dreams.

After the empowerment I went into strict retreat in a cave with my wife. Early on, she became very sick and left to go to the hospital in the nearest town, Mandi, and afterward moved to Kulu Manali, a region that was farther north and cooler, for the duration of my retreat. Friends accompanied her since my retreat commitments prevented me from doing so, and thus we were again separated for about eight months. This was not unusual—any wife of a Tibetan lama expects that her husband will at times be in retreat, even for years at a time—but it was difficult because of Karma's illness.

An elderly nun named Ani Dezom served me during this retreat, which outwardly was uneventful except for one occurrence. We were living on *tsampa* and not much else, and of course, as Tibetans, we were somewhat regretful that we had no meat. Mutton and goat meat were too expensive, and beef was unavailable because of the Hindu taboo against eating it. One foggy morning as I was sitting in my cave, however, I heard a loud "thumph!" Ani Dezom went out to investigate and came back reporting that a calf had fallen to its death at the mouth of our cave—fresh meat on our doorstep.

Nevertheless, for a day and a half we didn't consider eating it because if the Indians found out about it, we would jeopardize the whole Tibetan community. This calf seemed to be food for the wild dogs and vultures only, not for us. Yet because the dense fog prevented them from finding their feast, these creatures did not come.

At last, in the dark of the second night, temptation prevailed. "Maybe we should have some meat with our supper," I suggested and Ani-la agreed. I told her not to damage the bones and to slice through the skin as though her knife were fangs or talons. We cooked small pieces of the meat well in salt and butter, and it was preserved for six days. On the following morning the fog lifted and the vultures quickly removed the evidence.

This retreat allowed me to accomplish a practice that would be of profound significance to me, to the Tibetans I served as a lama and to my future students. Red Tara revealed herself to me in her full, fathomless compassion and wisdom, resplendent with qualities. I had many visionary experiences and dreams, some involving crystals. Two decades later I would remember these crystals and open the practice of crystal healing through Tara meditation. In the West, thousands of people would receive the blessing of Red Tara and begin to rely on Tara practice as their central Vajrayana meditation.

During part of the retreat I did one hundred thousand recitations of the "Essence of Interdependence" (Tendrel

177

Nyingpo), and at the completion of that practice I had a dream of the Buddha inseparable from the mountains, his head and torso an entire mountain with mantric syllables etched like gold relief on the rock cliffs. During another section of that retreat I did a Hayagriva practice that was a treasure discovered by one of the Tromge family lamas. The text had been left in Tibet, and I had forgotten it, but in retreat it returned to my memory in its entirety and afterward I wrote it down. Years later the original text was returned to me in Tibet.

When the retreat was over, I came down from the caves to the village, faced with the necessity of supporting Karma and myself, of settling somewhere and of establishing some sort of stable circumstances for our life together. I was invited to come to the Chamba region and serve the Tibetan road-workers there as a lama and a doctor, but when I announced my departure in Tso Pema, the news caused consternation among some of the Tibetans. Because I was the spokesperson designated by His Holiness, they felt that if I left, the group would lose cohesion. Yet I received no pay for my effort, and there really wasn't enough food or support for all of us in Tso Pema. When Karma joined me from Kulu Manali, a day's journey away, we decided to do roadwork. About eighty people joined us, and we headed toward Simla, the famous British hill station six hours from Tso Pema. On the way I spoke to the Indian government about giving the whole group work. The Indians saw me as a contractor and paid me a small finder's fee, and this began a whole series of misadventures.

Roadwork in India is backbreaking labor that involves chipping away the mountainsides with picks, breaking stones with sledge hammers, toting rock, shoveling, all for a few rupees a day. It was my job to keep the crew working, and it soon became plain to me that they were spiritual practitioners but not competent laborers. Any time someone wasn't staring directly at them, they sat down and began to drink tea and joke. In India cheap labor is always available, so when the road supervisors came to check on our progress and found practically none, they fired the whole lot of us, not worried in the least that this meant we wouldn't have money for food.

We were fired several times. I became increasingly distressed, not just because of the possibility of complete destitution if we couldn't earn our wages, but because of the lack of integration of spiritual practice with daily activity. The great *siddhas* of former times carried out the most ordinary activities—pounding sesame seeds into oil, blacksmithing, hoeing fields, casting clay pots—for years at a time, yet in each moment of their work their mind's awareness never moved. The ultimate result was revelation of the very nature of being. Our crew members would perform ceremonies, make offerings and cultivate altruistic motivation for hours each day, but when they stood up from their meditation they would go out and refuse to give their employer an honest day's work. I tried to talk about the need to integrate practice into every aspect of activity, but they couldn't see my point. They thought I was just trying to serve the Indian bosses and make my own money, without much thought to their welfare. I hit one of the lowest points of my life.

There were other difficulties as well. Everywhere we went, passports were required and since most of us didn't have them, *baksheesh* had to be given. We gave little bribes to the police of each district, handed over as friendly gifts to facilitate our journey. Without *baksheesh* we were subject to endless delays. Difficulties arose also because as meat eaters

179

in a predominantly vegetarian country, we were regarded as almost untouchable. Ironically, our surreptitious cooking of meat almost cost us our lives.

One night another lama and his wife were staying with Karma and me in a rented roadside room. We had a little charcoal brazier with which we were rendering meat fat on the sly because only vegetarian food was permitted. When we finished cooking, we went to sleep. It was a hot, stuffy night. I couldn't sleep well and finally went out to urinate. When I came back I left the door ajar to allow a bit of fresh air in the room. I slept a short time, but woke up again because the other lama's wife was groaning horribly, thrashing where she had fallen on the ground.

I flipped on the light and Karma leapt up to help, then she also crashed to the ground unconscious. The other lama, surmising that we had been attacked by a demon, jumped up in his bed and, clad only in his underwear, began to thunder wrathful mantras. All kinds of people came rushing to the door and demanded to know what had happened. I fumbled out, feeling quite dizzy. The other lama said he was dizzy, too. People were helping our wives, and they regained consciousness. Gradually the whole wild scene subsided and we all went back to bed.

The next morning our wives still were not feeling well, so we took them to the hospital. The doctor asked, "Did you have a charcoal fire in the room?"

"Yes."

"Then you were very lucky not to have died of asphyxiation. Many people perish from the carbon monoxide gas given off by charcoal when there is not proper ventilation."

Had I not left the door ajar, it is highly probable that we all would have died that night.

After I had traveled with the road crew for some months I received a letter from His Holiness Dudjom Rinpoche. He wrote that the Dalai Lama had recognized that Nyingma practitioners were scattered all over India and had suggested that they be amassed into a strong community. Dudjom Rinpoche himself had been trying to accomplish this with his plan to settle the Nyingmas in Padma Kod, but this had proved impossible. As an alternative to Padma Kod, the Indian government had offered a tract of land for seven hundred settlers in the eastern state of Orissa. Now His Holiness asked me to organize this settlement.

I didn't want to do it. I was weary and discouraged from the months with the road crew, which had expanded to a hundred and sixty persons relying on me. I had no enthusiasm for increasing my responsibilities in this way. My wife didn't want to go either. Orissa would be a farming settlement. She had grown up as a farmer's daughter in Tibet and knew the ceaseless demands the land would make. "It's better to work on the roads," she said, "then quit in the evening and sleep peacefully at night." She said that if I went she would go stay with her relatives. I wrote a letter to His Holiness explaining my reasons for declining.

A while later I received a second, extremely sad letter saying that His Holiness had asked a number of others and no one was willing to take responsibility for this project. I felt the weight of His Holiness's burden and the depth of his concern. It was impossible for me to decline again. I wrote him an acceptance and told Karma she was free to go to her relatives if she preferred, but she decided to stay with me after all. I organized the people, and three hundred prepared to go. They quit their work, packed up their belongings and waited in Simla until our departure.

At this point our plans fell apart. The Indian government had promised to reimburse us for our train fares when we arrived in Orissa; my Tibetan settlers did not trust this promise and wanted the government to prepay the tickets. The members of our group had money from their roadwork but refused to spend it on train tickets, asking me to tell the Indian officials that they were destitute and to negotiate. With strong misgivings, I contacted the Indian government, urging them to prepay our train tickets. We waited and waited, our funds dwindling as we camped doing nothing.

Finally the group decided it would be better to go on to Orissa, even if it meant risking not being reimbursed. They sent me to the Tibetan liaison for refugees and the Indian government. He offered no help, saying he had no information about Orissa from either Tibetan or Indian authorities, and made no suggestions as to how I should approach the Indian bureaucracy. I accepted the fact that he had no information, but it exasperated me that he refused to help us at all. I told him that if he really had no idea how to assist us, he needn't worry, I would take care of it myself.

I decided to go straight to the top, to contact the Indian minister of the interior. I called on a Tibetan acquaintance who worked in some low-level capacity in the offices of the Indian government and asked him for advice about how to contact the minister.

"You can't do that. As a refugee you can't go knocking on these people's doors. If you do, you can't expect them to talk to you." I thanked him for his advice and left.

As I passed a small office building in the government complex, I saw an Indian official typing furiously. He had a telephone. I introduced myself with my few words of Hindi, then went out and brought back a friend of mine who was fluent. We sat down and through the translator I told him the whole story, concluding with, "Now three hundred of us are here in Delhi, with no work, running out of money, waiting to go. Do you think I can call the minister of the interior?"

The Indian official replied testily, "Well, why not? The man is an agent of the government and his job is to help people. You have a problem, so why shouldn't you call him? I'll do it for you."

To this day I have no idea what this man's job was, but he picked up the telephone and got through to the minister himself. He was very snappy. "Three hundred Tibetans are here at your invitation and now you say don't come. What are they going to eat? Either they have to go to Orissa or you have to figure out a way to feed them here."

The minister said that we should go to Orissa right away. Everything was resolved. Gratefully I thanked the Indian for his help, which had more than solved our problem. It had given me confidence that I could work with the Indian government.

We traveled to Orissa by train, a four-day journey. We paid for our train tickets with the hope that our resettlement expenses would be reimbursed after our arrival at the camp, which, in fact, they were. Buses met us at the train station to take us to the campsite. We pulled in at night, and the next morning we were greeted by two Tibetan delegates appointed by the government-in-exile in Dharamsala to head the other two camps in the Orissa region.

As it happened, the Indian minister of the interior was making a tour of the Orissa region and visited our camp. He asked for me by name, and after we were introduced, he in turn introduced me to several other high Indian officials. He encouraged me to continue to make the needs of our camp known directly to the Indian government, which opened a very useful channel of influence and enabled me to sidestep unnecessary bureaucratic procedures.

This ability to accomplish things benefited the settlers in my camp, but it did not endear me to the other Tibetan officials, who distrusted me as a maverick. At one point a Tibetan official, a Nyingmapa fellow who was over the three of us who were camp administrators, actually went to Dharamsala and persuaded officials there to tangle me in procedures. Afterward I received a letter outlining a number of complicated procedures I was to follow, which I basically ignored.

As for the Indian officials with whom I worked on a day-to-day basis, I was very courteous and careful not to hurt their pride, for I could see that if they were wounded they would hold a grudge for a long time. Instead I extended good old-fashioned Khampa hospitality to them. Whenever they visited me I made them feel welcome and offered them the best I had. They were very appreciative of generosity and of being treated like friends, and they liked me particularly in comparison with some of the other Tibetan representatives, who treated them as incompetent servants. If there were any confusion, delay or mistake, these Tibetans would ring up their own superiors in Dharamsala, who would ring up Indian officials in Delhi, who would reprimand the Indian officials in Orissa, who would be resentful and even less cooperative.

Our first resettlement job was to make the existing mud houses livable and to divide and till the land for farming. Orissa is jungle terrain, and although trees had been cut, creating tillable fields required a monumental amount of hard work. Even in populous India no one had been willing to do this work before. Fortunately, the same people who had balked at roadwork were willing to give full effort to the settlement. The Indian government supported us with gifts of food for three years, and afterward our fields and gardens prospered. Our cash crops were corn, potatoes, peanuts and pineapples.

One evening an Indian official came to me and said, "Tomorrow a Swiss fellow is coming to talk with you about setting up a carpet factory in your camp. This is an opportunity for prosperity. This fellow has already been to another camp where he hoped to locate the factory, but they told him they had no wool spinners or weavers, so he left disappointed."

I was very grateful for the tip, and had cookies and tea to offer the Swiss man when he arrived the next day. He worked for a Swiss economic assistance program for refugees. We talked for a while; then he asked, "Are there any weavers in this camp who know how to make traditional Tibetan carpets?"

"Yes, a few." I was thinking of the one person who knew how to weave. "We have about thirty weavers here," I said, now thinking of thirty possibilities.

"How many people know how to spin wool?"

"Almost every Tibetan woman knows how to spin, so you could say we have almost two hundred spinners."

He was very pleased, and that afternoon he marked a plot for the carpet factory building. The next day he brought in a labor force to begin construction. The Swiss are quite diligent and efficient.

Meanwhile, I was also very busy constructing a labor force. In a far corner of the camp my one weaver began giving classes to thirty others. They pulled apart sweaters so that they would have wool to use and built temporary looms to practice on. In four months the factory was complete, a fine building with offices and big workrooms. Also in four months thirty weavers and one hundred and ninety spinners were trained and ready to work. The carpet factory became a major source of prosperity for our community.

DURING OUR TIME in Orissa, Karma gave birth to our son, Jigmed Ngawang Norbu. As with our first son who had died, I had a series of unusual and auspicious dreams about the time of Jigmed's birth. Before his conception I had a dream of an Indian *sadhu,* a wandering yogi, approaching and handing me a small Tibetan-style book. He spoke to me in Tibetan, saying, "You should keep this." Opening the book, I saw that the first half appeared to be written in Sanskrit, and the second half was a Tibetan translation of the Sanskrit.

Later, during Karma's pregnancy, she and I had a dream on the same night of this Indian *sadhu.* In my dream, he held in his hands a sacred water bowl and sprinkled water throughout our house. In Karma's dream, he offered her a mirror and an arrow, sliding the arrow underneath her blouse toward her chest. On the actual night of Jigmed's conception in Orissa I had a lucid dream of a young Sikh man coming into our tent.

Just before Jigmed's birth, I dreamed of a warrior in full regalia—armor, a helmet and a sword, carrying a shield and a bow and arrow—who appeared to be Gesar, the eleventh-century dharma king. He said, "This is your son," and by this I understood that in some transcendent sense he had conferred a child on me. Our son was born on the tenth day of the eleventh month of the Dragon Year.

186

My fullest, most auspicious dream occurred when Jigmed was a young boy. In that dream I went to Zangdog Palri, Glorious Copper-Colored Mountain, the pureland of Padmasambhava, to take part in a great offering ceremony and to ask Padmasambhava who my son was. However, upon arrival I didn't have the audacity to enter Padmasambhava's presence, so I began circumambulating his celestial palace along with a great gathering of realization holders and *dakinis*. Suddenly I came across my mother. She had a very white complexion with a bluish tinge. She laughed when she saw me and before I could speak she said, "Your son is Yudra Nyingpo." Yudra Nyingpo was one of the twenty-five close disciples of Padmasambhava who was renowned as a *siddha,* a translator and a master of the Great Perfection. Karma and I rejoiced in the birth of this son.

I WAS IN ORISSA for three years, as lama, doctor, administrator. It was a satisfying time and I was proud of the people, of how much they had accomplished by their hard work. Yet in the end there was disappointment as well, when small-minded sectarianism divided the practitioners of two Nyingma lineages. I held both lineages, had practiced both very thoroughly, had tested the methods of both and had found them as pure as gold and in essence the same. I did not see the camp as the exclusive practice domain of one or the other, and I myself practiced with both groups.

It disturbed me deeply, then, when representatives of the predominant group came to me and said they thought it detrimental that there were two practice groups. I didn't say much, but I went to His Holiness Dudjom Rinpoche and asked, "If some people have been practicing according to one lineage, is it necessary for them to change lineages in order to create unity in the community?"

His Holiness responded vigorously. "Certainly not. Whatever practice a person is well grounded in is what he should continue. Part of our purpose is to preserve all lineages as methods for attaining enlightenment."

His answer pleased and assured me because that is how I understood the dharma. I returned to Orissa and continued to support both groups. Though I didn't make a strong speech, I did indicate that there was nothing contradictory or disharmonious in the essence of the two lineages, and that as practitioners we should sustain our own tradition while respecting and rejoicing in the virtue of other traditions.

However, I didn't sense that my words held sway and once again, as after the months with the road crew, I experienced profound weariness. In my heart I knew the time had come to leave Orissa.

11

Partings

I TRAVELED to Tso Pema, leaving Karma and our son Jigmed Norbu, now two years old, behind until I could establish a new situation for us. His Holiness Dudjom Rinpoche was giving another series of empowerments in Tso Pema, and while I attended these, I had the opportunity to speak with him privately. I told him I had done what I could in Orissa and things were prospering, but now some were antagonized by my style of administration and my management of dharma activities. I asked to resign before these antagonisms, which at this point were focused on me personally, flared into real divisions in the camp.

About this time a nun gave a monastery to His Holiness in the Chamba district and requested that a lama come there. Because of the extreme isolation and poverty of the area, it was not a sought-after assignment. I asked His Holiness if I might go; he agreed and offered me a stipend, which I did not accept. Thus began a three-year interlude in which events presented themselves with special drama amid the utter austerity of our circumstances and the thin, rare atmosphere of the high Himalayas.

The monastery was splendidly located in the mountains north of Dalhousie, a British colonial hill station in the western Himalayas, and five miles from a little village named Titsa. At that time the monastery was eighteen miles from the nearest bus stop, and for several winter months the steep, rocky path to Titsa was almost impassable because of heavy snow and avalanches.

Karma, Jigmed Norbu, an attendant named Tashi and I lived in a house near the small monastery. Our daughter, Dawa Lhamo, was born in Chamba. My salary consisted of three small bags of barley and some potatoes. This was supplemented by the small offerings people gave for specific ceremonies. At times it seemed as if the basic needs of our little household would not be met, and Karma worried and blamed me. The strains in our marriage first became apparent during this time. I always had confidence that at least we would not be hungry and cold, and I was relatively content. In fact, we always did have just enough, but Karma, who did not have the same confidence, often found our frugal existence stressful and uncomfortable.

In winter we had to be very cautious about the hunters who came through, and one day we refused to give shelter to a group who seemed especially unsavory. Though they left, we felt they might retaliate. I knew a ceremony for averting such negativity, but it required a certain animal horn, which would be impossible to find with the ground buried in deep snow. As we were considering what to do, my dog, a white, fluffy little thing, appeared with just the right type of horn.

We began to prepare for the ceremony, but as we were careless about the horn, the dog took it away and buried it again. A heavy snow fell and continued for three days. When the snowfall finally stopped, we climbed onto the roof of the monastery to shovel off the load. The dog went out too and began to dig furiously. Triumphantly, she laid bare her horn. We borrowed it from her once more and performed the ceremony. Hunters never troubled us again.

One summer I was acutely sick with what had been a strange, chronic stomach disorder. I could eat solids but even a single cup of liquid made me feel extremely uncomfortable. A friend asked a man who was said to be an amazing oracle to visit me. The oracle arrived wearing ordinary clothes and appeared to be a rather ordinary Tibetan. I thought he would do some simple form of divination, but unexpectedly, he started shaking and going into a trance. Suddenly a thunderous voice boomed forth, demanding, "Zhonnu Tonely, why did you summon me?" Then the oracle came out of the trance and promised to return in a few days to treat me.

The second time he visited he wore the full regalia of an oracle—an elaborate headdress, an ornate brocade robe, bone ornaments—and his appearance was very impressive. He performed extensive prayers and ceremonies, then shaking, he entered a trance. Using a white *katag* to form a silken tube, he held one end to my stomach and the other to his mouth. Then he sucked hard and spit into a cup several times until the cup was half-filled with a black, gelatinous, poisonous-looking substance. Still in this trance state, he explained that I had been poisoned in a restaurant long before, though it wasn't clear whether I was poisoned deliberately by an enemy or accidentally by food. Somewhat to my surprise, this bizarre method actually alleviated my stomach ailment.

After I felt better I traveled around the Chamba region, performing ceremonies in people's homes and teaching, particularly *p'howa*. A distraught woman began to come to many of my sessions, and in a private interview, she begged me to transfer her consciousness out of her body because, she said, she could not continue to live in the presence of her cruel daughter-in-law. Of course, this was an improper request—it was like asking me to facilitate her suicide—but she was so persistent that finally I felt it necessary to respond so that people wouldn't think there was no power in *p'howa* practice.

"If that is what you really want," I told her, "tomorrow I will come to your son's house and transfer your consciousness to the pureland." The next day we both sat in meditation posture. I did the practice with great strength for about a half hour. The woman was becoming dizzy and somewhat dazed when suddenly she interrupted the practice. "May I go get a drink of water?" she asked.

"Yes, certainly," I replied.

She went into the kitchen, slipped out the back door and never came back. Afterward she went around the village saying that it was the wrong season to die, there would be no flowers for her grave, so she would have to wait for a different season. Few people look into death's abyss and really want to jump.

One day, during my last winter in the Chamba region, I walked the five miles down to Titsa to attend to some business. Before I could return, avalanches blocked the road, so I stayed overnight in a restaurant. That night I dreamed that I was flying high over the earth, and looking down I could see people everywhere. I sang the mantra of Padmasambhava as I flew and carried a skullcup filled with *dutzi*, the nectar of blessing. A voice from the sky said, "Whoever hears your song will not be reborn in hell; whoever tastes your *dutzi* will likewise be spared."

The next day, since the roads were still blocked by snow, I

went to a nearby monastery and assisted the monks by doing some ornamental painting. I also took the opportunity to make *dutzi* with a mixture of consecrated substances and *chang*. For many days I performed ceremonies and recited prayers, until nectar overflowed from the skullcup, saturated the cotton on which it rested and filled the room with an unusual sweet smell—the indications of successful practice.

After three years I felt it was time to leave Chamba. I had not accomplished much there. The people liked me but they had no leisure to practice during good-weather months because they worked hard in the fields. In the winter, they were inaccessible. Moreover, the main motivation of many of them for following Buddhism was their belief that it would protect them from black magic, which was widely practiced and feared in that area. They would come to me with stories of strange phenomena that they traced back to some person who hated or envied them. I did not deny the authenticity of their experiences, and usually, if I performed a *chod* ceremony, the phenomena abated. Still, even though they were grateful and awed, these people were not interested in methods for taming their own minds or in seeing that their own fear and negativity had provided the stage for demonic appearances. I felt that I could help them in the moment but could not effect long-term change.

To clear my leaving Chamba with His Holiness Dudjom Rinpoche, I traveled to Darjeeling in a full arc across India to the eastern Himalayas. Dudjom Rinpoche was not home, but I met and explained my position to his wife, Sangyum Rigdzin Wangmo, who gave me permission to leave.

On my return, I completely ran out of money in the capital of the Chamba district. Since I needed only eighteen rupees (about $2.25) for the bus ticket, I went to a Tibetan family I knew and asked for a loan. They regretted that they couldn't loan me any money because they were goldsmiths and had that very day spent all their currency on gold. I thanked them and left.

I went back to the stalls by the bus stop, trying to decide what to do. A Pakistani merchant in one of the stalls asked me where I was going. I told him I was on my way home but had no money for my ticket. He said, "I'll give you the money," and he handed me twenty rupees. I thanked him and promised to repay him, but he said, "As you like, one way or the other." I did repay him, and I have never forgotten his kindness.

Karma and I decided to move to Bir, a Tibetan settlement in the foothills of the Himalayas, about a half-day's bus trip from Dharamsala, the residence of the Dalai Lama. Bir was on a plateau and was surrounded by fields that extended toward the mountains. Most its two thousand inhabitants were Khampas from Dege and Nangchhen who knew me, at least by name.

As usual I traveled ahead of my family to make living arrangements, although this time I brought my son Jigmed, who was about five years old. On the day Karma and my daughter Dawa were supposed to arrive, I woke up with a deep sense of foreboding that followed me all morning. I happened to meet a young lama named Urgyen Topgyal, the son of the great Chhöling Rinpoche, and told him I felt disturbed, but for no particular reason.

Urgyen Topgyal said, "We should do *puja* right away." He summoned the monks of Chhöling Gonpa to help with the preparations and to participate. Our prayers and the ceremony alleviated my anxiety, but it had not been unfounded. When Karma and Dawa arrived in the afternoon, I learned that their jeep had collided with another vehicle on the mountain road below Dalhousie and it was extremely fortunate that there had been no fatalities or major injuries. Dawa's forehead was cut, but only superficially.

The presence of Chhöling Rinpoche ("Chhö-ling" being the abbreviation of Chhögyur Lingpa) greatly enhanced my stay in Bir. My connection with the Chhöling lineage began after my first three-year retreat in Tibet, when my stepfather asked Sechhen Rabjam to determine my main practice in this lifetime. Sechhen Rabjam responded by empowering me into a Tara treasure that had been revealed by the first Chhögyur Lingpa, who had lived in the nineteenth century. Over the years I received other Chhöling empowerments and much later, in Tso Pema, I met Chhöling Rinpoche, who gave me the empowerment for his treasure named the *Tukdrup Barché Kunsel* (*Mind Practice for Dispelling All Obstacles*) and for Tseringma, an important dharma protector.

The connection that had begun to be forged by these empowerments in Tso Pema grew stronger in Bir, where we often performed ceremonies together. I revered Chhöling Rinpoche as one of the great lamas of the Nyingma tradition, and I liked him personally, for his warmth, his dignity and the equanimity of his expansive mind. There was not a trace of pettiness about him, and he constantly demonstrated the qualities of a *siddha,* impossible to fathom in an ordinary way. One day, for example, during an extensive *drubchhen* ceremony in which he was the *vajra* master, he appeared to fall asleep on his throne. Afterward he described a vision he had had in which all the local deities and guardians of Sikkim approached him and requested that he give them a place to stay. This assembly said that the king of Sikkim had been "asleep" for three years, meaning that he had been somehow negligent or inattentive. "Things must be pretty bad in Sikkim," Chhöling Rinpoche commented. Politically, certainly they were, for the Indian government, fearful that Sikkim might be a weak point on its border with China, had stationed troops there and thoroughly undermined the autonomy of the Sikkimese government.

Chhöling Rinpoche died suddenly in a jeep accident while I was in Bir. I grieved over this loss, for he had been a source of pure dharma. At the same time I experienced another loss, for my marriage was collapsing. It seemed ironic that this should happen now in Bir, where we were relatively comfortable, and after we had already weathered long separations, the death of our first child, sickness and financial hardship.

There are many contributing causes, both obvious and subtle, for the disintegration of any relationship, and one cannot say, "This is why . . ." without oversimplifying. From my perspective, I think Karma lost hope that I would develop the kind of ambition that would lift our family out of impoverishment. She could not even convince me that we were impoverished, and this frustrated her. An excellent businesswoman herself, she admired people who did business and who actively worked to increase their family's circumstances. For her it was probably unbearable to think that our family's lot might never improve because I was content with it. There were arguments and reconciliations, with the arguments striking deeper and the reconciliations becoming shallower. Finally, I moved out of the house and, shortly after, to Delhi. Tibetans rarely divorce, so our separation caused something of a scandal.

In years to come, Karma and I would occasionally correspond in regard to our children and I would send her money as I could, but we never saw each other again. As long as there was a karmic basis for our relationship, no amount of adversity could sever it; when our karmic connection ceased to exist, no amount of longing could reestablish it. All this was extremely painful for me and for my children, especially Jigmed, who was older. Although Jigmed sometimes lived with me and we remained close, the separation completely disrupted my relationship with my daughter Dawa Lhamo, who stayed with her mother. We would see each other only once—a two-day visit—in the next fifteen years.

I drank a lot of *arak* in Delhi and wrote a long poem about impermanence. A friend read it and wept, borrowed and mislaid it, so even that remembrance was gone.

IN DELHI I embarked on a long, tedious process to obtain a visa to the United States. One summer I had left Bir and gone to Kulu Manali, a cool place in the mountains. Many Tibetans were there and I began teaching some of them. Out of that came an invitation from the Dalai Lama to go to the United States and teach, contingent on my finding a translator and obtaining a visa. I had no special desire to go to the United States then, although I remembered my dream about "America" when I first arrived in India and took it as a sign that I might go there. Also, in Bir I began meeting Western Buddhists.

Among the first Westerners I met were two Canadians who had taken Tibetan dharma names, Shakya Dorje and Tamchö, and who spoke fluent Tibetan. I also met some Americans, Howard Davidson, Jocelyn Sylvester and Jon and Lynn Weinberger. I formed enduring friendships with all of them, and Jocelyn and Jon later became close students. I liked the alert minds of these people, their humor and their generosity. They asked good questions and seemed to have genuine faith in and respect for the dharma. Some Tibetans warned me not to become involved with Westerners, saying they were not loyal students and went around from lama to lama, never really applying what they heard. That has not been my general experience, and over the years I have encountered Western students whom any lama would value as pure holders of their lineage.

The visa process continued for more than three years with no success, and finally the Dalai Lama's representative suggested that I let the matter drop. As it turned out, this was a very good suggestion since the sponsor that had been found for me, a Texan, turned out to be an ill-motivated charlatan who wanted to indenture a lama to give credibility to his fraudulent religious activities. Later I would learn that he was indicted by the U.S. government for his activities.

Meanwhile I established a life in Delhi. It was the first city I had lived in since Lhasa, and it was much bigger than Lhasa. For a while I lived with a large family from Nyagrong, then I moved to Majnukatilla, a Tibetan camp on the banks of the Jamuna River. Here were the poorest Tibetans. They lived in tents, and occasionally the Jamuna would flood and wash out the camp. Nevertheless, it was a pleasant place to be, particularly because I did not encounter much of the sectarianism or political conflict common in the other camps. We built a small *lha khang* (temple) there, and practitioners from all four traditions used it. I also helped make a Padmasambhava statue for the shrine.

However, I almost died from malaria while I was in Delhi. A family I knew well summoned me to perform ceremonies for a young woman in their family who had passed away. I was not feeling well myself, but they implored me to come. I began the ceremonies, then asked the monk who was assisting me to carry on while I lay down. He could not finish the section, so I got up, with a shattering headache and sweat pouring down my face, and completed the recitation. Then I lay down again and could not get up for days. The family brought a number of doctors to examine me, but none diagnosed malaria. At last I had a dream of going to a certain hospital and finding help. When I described the dream to the people taking care of me, they took me to the hospital. The entrance was indeed the same as it had been in my dream. The doctor on duty examined me and said, "Sir, you have malaria and I think I can help you. Please take these capsules." If we had arrived even thirty minutes later, I think I surely would have died. Within hours after I had taken the medicine, my fever abated and I began to recover my strength. My friends notified the doctor, who was surprised and delighted.

After my recovery, I had a dream in which a black horse prostrated before me, entreating me to remain at the Majnu-katilla camp. I did not understand the full meaning of the dream, but immediately many people from the camp began to ask me to recite prayers and perform ceremonies for them. I remained there for several months, until the fall of 1977, when I left India for Boudhanath, Nepal, to receive all of the empowerments for the Dudjom treasures from His Holiness Dudjom Rinpoche. As I left, I had no inkling that it would be nine years before I would return to India, and that my return would be under very different circumstances.

12

Nepal

THE DUDJOM EMPOWERMENTS given by His Holiness
Dudjom Rinpoche—and the Chhöling Tersar empowerments given by His Holiness Khyentse Rinpoche
afterward—were great occasions in Tibetan Buddhism,
attended by at least one hundred and fifty lamas and ten
times that many lay persons. As the assembly gathered in the
huge shrineroom of Tulku Urgyen's monastery, we Tibetans
could assess how well we had held the jewels of dharma when
we had crossed the Tibetan border otherwise empty-handed
eighteen years before. Clearly the relevance of the dharma
was undiminished, as evidenced, in part, by the many
Westerners attending the empowerments. They represented
the expanding horizons of Vajrayana since its departure from
the isolation of Tibet.

Also present were the young incarnations of Chhögyur
Lingpa, Jamyang Khyentse Chhökyi Lodrö and others of the
new generation of *tulkus*. My eleven-year-old son Jigmed,
whom I had not seen in the two years since I left Bir, was also
among this energetic group of boys. Chhöling Rinpoche had
said in Bir that Jigmed was an incarnation of Tsewang Norbu,

the son of the first Chhögyur Lingpa in the last century. These young *tulkus* gave a sense of joyful renewal to the proceedings.

Attending the empowerments was Lama Ladakh Nono, an old lama from Western Tibet who was famous for being able to foretell future events by looking into a mirror and psychically seeing in the letters that arose answers to specific questions. Now he did such a divination for me, writing down what he saw. He said that I would go to the West and benefit many people there by teaching the dharma, but he warned that several persons who had had a bad relationship with me in former lives—who had broken their sacred commitment, or *samaya*—had taken rebirth in the West and some difficulties would arise.

He also predicted that a Western woman named Chhökyi Drolma would come into my life and that this would be good. One day, as I was sitting in Khyentse Rinpoche's empowerments, I looked back across the aisle and noticed a Western woman. She was surrounded by a red radiance, not a fleeting light, but powerful and compelling. She sat in the same place each day thereafter, and one morning she offered me a jar of honey. I invited her to have lunch with me in Jigmed's and my room in the monastery. She spoke no Tibetan and I spoke only a few words of English, so our communication was minimal, but I learned that her Western name was Jane and her dharma name Chhökyi Drolma. I did not remember the name from the mirror divination until a month or so later when I was rummaging around my room and found the notes that Lama Nono had written. By that time my relationship with Jane had progressed to the point that we had discussed my traveling to the United States with her.

Though I did not mention the red radiance until years later, I told her about the prediction of the mirror divination, adding, "There are many women in the Tibetan dharma with the name Chhökyi Drolma." By this time, however, Jane had requested her own divination from His Eminence Tai Situ Rinpoche. Tai Situ had told her that she would marry me and there would be four or five years of difficulty, but then the marriage would be extremely good.

After the empowerments Jigmed resumed his studies at an institute for Buddhist philosophy directed by Khetsun Zangpo Rinpoche, a renowned Nyingma scholar. Though at least eight years younger than the other students, he did very well and I was pleased with him. When he was settled in school, I began a short retreat in a house outside of Boudhanath. An Englishwoman who had taken vows as a Tibetan Buddhist nun did a retreat in the house at the same time, and Jane offered to serve both of us by marketing and cooking.

The retreat was the first extended time I had spent with Jane; during it I simply observed her and rarely criticized. She had some qualities I appreciated—she was devoted, generous and extremely hard-working, and we shared many humorous moments together. However, I also saw that she could be short-tempered, willful and very unskillful in her speech even when her intentions were good.

After a few months Jane left Nepal and toured India with her mother. Then she returned to Nepal overland, bringing all my books and belongings from Delhi. Ours was not an easy reunion, because my instinct was to show her everything that could be difficult between us instead of prolonging the easygoing acquiescence of the initial months of our re-lationship. Where before I mostly focused on her good qualities, now I criticized her faults and triggered her negative emotions, particularly her anger. She in turn had the full opportunity to discover the downside of life with me—that I would be constantly demanding, that there would be little privacy, that there would be uncertainty in my health and financial situation and that personal needs would often be shunted aside in favor of the needs of others.

My behavior was not calculated, but it certainly established an arena where we could test the mettle of our relationship, which proved surprisingly resilient. Conflicts did not result in seething resentment and long-standing grudges. The black moments seemed to disperse like storm clouds. Jane was committed to the dharma, and from the very beginning she viewed our relationship more in terms of a teacher–student relationship than an ordinary love affair. Even when we argued or she was unhappy about a turn of events, she was fairly quick to check her motivation, acknowledge any flaws in it and try to accommodate my wishes as her teacher. I respected this and I began to have more faith in the enduring nature of our relationship, in the karmic bond between us. Still, it would take years more—four or five, just as Tai Situ had prophesied—before our connection fully flourished.

ONE DAY after the retreat, His Holiness Dudjom Rinpoche summoned me to his home in Kathmandu. I arrived, prostrated before him, and after we exchanged greetings, he said, "Why don't you visit me more often?"

"In India," I replied, "I had more opportunity to work with you directly and to ask your advice about the Nyingma communities and centers. Now I don't have a formal connection to this work, and so I don't have this excuse to call on you."

I should have stopped there, but I didn't. "A second reason I don't come is that your attendants are very rude. No matter who comes, they don't pay them any attention. In fact, they don't even look at people, much less assist them in seeing you. If people make requests of you, your attendants don't bring back the answer. Instead they set up a wall between you and your visitors.

"I myself am a bad man with a bad temper, and when they are rude, I am angry. I leave, and then I have much regret. I remind myself that these attendants are my *vajra* brothers, that we share the same teacher, that I'm at fault for not having a pure view of them. On the other hand, I'm realistic and I know that if I encounter their rudeness again, I'll probably lose my temper again, so there is no point in coming around and creating negative karma and making a bother."

At this His Holiness laughed merrily for a long time. He didn't reply to what I had said, but when he stopped laughing, he said, "I need a lama to go to Orissa, to Kalimpong, to France or to America. In Orissa, particularly, many people have told me that you were very kind and a good teacher. Things went well there, and you might want to consider returning."

I told him, "It wasn't easy working for the Nyingma communities and centers. I had to resolve many difficult problems and I tried to do so without disturbing you or your wife, Sangyum Kushog. In Orissa, especially, some of your students had their own way of doing things and it was by no means easy to be their leader. I would go back there only if you told me to directly, but otherwise I would rather not."

His Holiness was very gracious. He simply said, "Well, think about it. And also, if you decide to go to the West, we will help you with a visa and an airplane ticket." I declined the offer, saying that at present I didn't need help but I would inform him if things changed. Then he called his wife and she gave me a beautiful piece of Bhutanese cloth, a Bhutanese jacket and some other gifts to acknowledge my previous efforts. His Holiness reiterated his offer to help with a visa and ticket and again I declined.

To be in Dudjom Rinpoche's personal presence was always pure joy. During my stay in Nepal I received empowerments and oral transmissions for all the treasures he had discovered in this life and in his previous life as Dudjom Lingpa. It was a wealth of practices whose splendor is unsurpassed, and deep within me I formed the aspiration to offer this transmission to others, through empowerment and teaching.

HIS HOLINESS KHYENTSE RINPOCHE'S empowerments into the Chhögyur Lingpa treasures followed His Holiness Dudjom Rinpoche's. Before the empowerments each day, I organized the texts for Khyentse Rinpoche. By now I had a very warm relationship with him, and the closer I became, the more I admired him. He had the best Khampa style of conversation, direct with a wonderful sense of humor, though listening to him give discourses on the dharma was like hearing the deity Manjushri himself—the very essence of intelligence—speak. His personal needs were very simple. He cared nothing about clothes, for example, but again in the best Khampa style, he wore a gold *gau* and gold and diamond rings.

In years to come, when I encountered serious obstacles to my health and even to my life, Khyentse Rinpoche appeared to me in visions and encouraged me to overcome these obstacles. His blessings were unobstructed by time and space, like the radiance of a universal sun.

JANE AND I moved into two rented rooms on the main street in Boudhanath. The heart of Boudha is not its main street, but the immense white *stupa* built before the time of Padmasambhava. Every day, morning and evening especially, hundreds of people circumambulated the *stupa*. Such circumambulation offered a powerful opportunity for meditation, particularly on impermanence and the spontaneous arising of phenomenal events.

My days in Boudha had a certain rhythm. I would awaken at five, and by six my sitting room would be filled with people requesting advice, divination or diagnosis of an illness by a Tibetan pulse reading. At eight o'clock I would go to some private home where I would conduct ceremonies the family had requested. I would return in the evening about six, and my room would again be filled with people, not just Tibetans and Westerners, but Nepalis, both Hindu and Buddhist. After dinner I would teach a group of Westerners the preliminary practices (*ngondro*) of Tibetan Vajrayana, speaking in Tibetan to a young man named Ngodrup, who translated it into English. The translation was not perfect because Ngodrup was still learning English, and dharma concepts and vocabulary are not easy to convey even for a native speaker. Ngodrup was highly intelligent and very persistent, however, and my Western students were patient and adaptable listeners, so I believe they received some benefit from the teaching.

IN JULY 1979, Jane left Nepal to stay in Japan for a few months before returning to the United States. I spent the next four months engaged in the tedious process of obtaining a passport and applying for a U.S. visa. As I waited, other events seemed rather insignificant compared with the possibility of visiting America. Many obstacles had been overcome. Plane tickets had been offered to me and to my translator Ngodrup, who would accompany and help me. An old friend, Howard Davidson, had offered his place in San Francisco. Jane sent me some money for traveling expenses and was ready to meet me at a moment's notice. Most important, however, some transition had been made in my mind. Having first heard the name "America" in a dream nineteen years before, shortly after I left Tibet, I was now ready to find out if I really had a karmic connection there and if I could bring about benefit. Also, my Western students had given fascinating descriptions of the technological capabilities and cultural oddities of the United States, and I wanted to see them for myself. After many months of waiting, I was granted a U.S. visa, and on the evening of October 24, 1979, Ngodrup and I arrived in California, touching down briefly in Los Angeles, where Jane, looking rather pale after four months in Tokyo, and Howard Davidson met me. We flew together to San Francisco and celebrated our arrival by drinking California brandy and talking for hours. At midnight we reset the clocks, for that was the autumn night that the time changed.

13

Return to Tibet

ONE DAY in 1982 a letter from my sister T'hrinlay Wangmo arrived at my home in Cottage Grove, Oregon. She had sent it with a Tibetan pilgrim who traveled from Kham to Nepal, and against all odds the fellow had found someone in Boudhanath who had an address for me. That it reached me was all the more remarkable in that I had lived in several places in the United States and had never left a forwarding address.

The letter was very brief. My sister said she was alive and wanted to see me. Tibetans consider short and terse to be good style for correspondence, but I regretted every word that she hadn't written about her life since I had last seen her more than thirty years before. Tears flooded my eyes. After so many separations and relocations, the compelling bond of a blood relationship had suddenly reconnected me to my homeland.

Yet in 1982 it seemed impossible to go back because of both the political situation in Tibet and my own situation in the United States. The Chinese, in an effort to woo the Dalai Lama back as a figurehead, had allowed several fact-finding delegations appointed by the Dalai Lama to travel in the "Autonomous Region of Tibet." The Tibetan people met the delegations with such an emotional outpouring of faith and devotion toward the Dalai Lama and showed such obvious distress about their condition that the Chinese were horrified. The years of communist indoctrination and the sham of material progress could not repress the Tibetans' longing for spiritual and cultural freedom. In defiance of government and military directives, thousands surged around the delegates wherever they went and made their stories known while the Chinese stood by, momentarily helpless.

The Chinese themselves were in a period of transition that began with Mao Zedong's decline in power and his death in 1976 and with the subsequent repudiation of the "gang of four," who had instigated a decade of brutal upheaval with the Cultural Revolution. Tentative attempts were made to decrease the country's isolation, and accordingly more tourists were allowed to visit China and Tibet, although at first in both places they were allowed to travel only in organized tours to specified destinations. Eastern Tibet, which the Chinese considered an enclave of unregenerate, barbaric reactionaries, was not among those destinations.

My personal situation also hindered me from journeying to Tibet at that time. I had not yet been granted a "green card" for permanent resident's status in the United States, making foreign travel very complicated if I wished to continue living there, which I did. From the beginning I felt at home in America, first in California and then in Oregon, where some very receptive students had gathered around me. I had given them empowerment for Red Tara and other important lineage treasures, and it was a pleasure to watch the dharma flourish in their minds. In 1982, my students, who had been organized

209

mainly under the auspices of Yeshe Nyingpo, the Dudjom centers in America, had requested that I establish Chagdud Gonpa in the West as the seat of the Chagdud incarnations. This request seemed to indicate that a strong, enduring foundation might be created for my teachings in the West and I gave it serious consideration.

Meanwhile, however, I was fully occupied with learning English, training my small group of students and carrying out a series of art projects. By the fall of 1982, I had sculpted—with the help of my students, some of whom were very fine artists—a small Guru Rinpoche, an over-life-sized Red Tara and a twenty-two-foot-high Guru Rinpoche. We had also built several shrines and an elaborate ceremonial throne and had begun the renovation of a large, dilapidated house that we used as our center. My students were excellent workers, and work became a mode of training.

I wrote my sister, asking her to meet me in Nepal and enclosing some money. There was no response. Later I would learn that the letter, carefully addressed by a friend who knew Chinese, actually reached my sister, although most of the money had been dissipated by the exchange rate and fees of the Chinese bank. My sister was unwilling to travel to Nepal because of the arduous trip and the difficulty of obtaining the requisite travel documents.

Not until five years later, in August 1987, was I able to return to Tibet. During the interim the Chinese had allowed many individual tourists into the Lhasa region and a number of lamas, including His Holiness Khyentse Rinpoche, had visited their monasteries in Eastern Tibet. By then I had my green card and had traveled extensively in foreign countries as well as the United States. I did have some concern about going back, however, because of repeated dreams of being seized by the Chinese military in Tibet and thrown into prison. Often the dreams ended with me asking myself, "Why did I come back here?" The opportunity to have a divination done by His Eminence Tai Situ Rinpoche arose, and he told me that if I sponsored the reading of certain texts and carried out several other dharma activities the journey would go well. I did all he advised and I felt confident.

Jane and I flew to Hong Kong, and my son Jigmed Norbu, coming from India, met us there. It was a very happy reunion, for I had been with Jigmed only one other time—during a two-month visit to Nepal and India—since immigrating to the United States. We flew together to Chengdu, the capital of Szechuan, where we were met by the "Tibetan Reception Committee," a group of Tibetans who worked within the Chinese government and made recommendations as to who should and should not receive special permits to enter Kham.

In retrospect the process of obtaining our permits as "homecoming Chinese" was smooth and easy, though our experience at the time was very uncertain, especially for Jane, who, with her blue eyes and brown hair, looked less Chinese than Jigmed or I. In the course of our meetings, various members of the Reception Committee warned me repeatedly not to teach, not to give empowerments and not to make any formal recognition of *tulkus*. In Chengdu this injunction was conveyed in a pleasant manner; later, in Kanting and other places, the tone became more menacing. One committee-woman told me, in an ominous voice, "You have come well; you will want to leave equally well."

To save the expense of hiring a jeep, we decided to travel by bus from Chengdu to Kanze, four days away. We had thousands of dollars stashed in bulging money belts under our clothes, wanting to offer as much of this as possible to the

monasteries. Thus at five one morning we took a taxi to the
Chengdu bus station, a cavernous concrete building where
hundreds of people milled around in the gray light and
loudspeakers blared constantly. Suddenly I noticed five
Tibetan monks making their way across the station, their gold
and maroon robes standing out in the drab surroundings. I
was wearing informal robes, and as soon as they noticed me
they came over and bowed their heads for a blessing. By
extraordinary coincidence they turned out to be monks from
Chagdud Gonpa, returning from a pilgrimage to Wu Tai
Shan, one of the most sacred Buddhist sites in China and a
place I intended to take my Western students when I came
out of Tibet.

The news of Chagdud Gonpa was wonderful. The monastery remained one of the few in Kham that had not been
destroyed. The texts and statues, hidden for decades, had
been returned to the monastery with only one small statue
lost. Three lamas had held Chagdud Gonpa in my absence,
and all three were now at the monastery training the monks.
There were only one hundred and thirty monks, about the
same number as before the Chinese took over, but in 1987
this made Chagdud Gonpa the second largest monastery in
Kham, as well as, the monks assured me, one of the best.
Although we traveled on separate buses, I saw the monks
often at rest stops during the next two days. At the old border
town of Kanting, however, we parted until I reached Chagdud
Gonpa. From Kanting to Kanze we followed the road the
Chinese army built to invade Tibet, the road where I first saw
a fleet of motorized vehicles and naively laughed, thinking
that they looked like a herd of pigs. Now, as I traveled this
road that had conveyed so much tragedy to Tibet, I was a
tourist in my own country, excited at the first sight of a yak, a

Tibetan magpie, a prayer wheel, taking landscape shots from the rattling bus with my little point-and-shoot camera, ignoring Jane when she said they could not possibly turn out well.

In Kanze we hired a vehicle and driver to take us to Tenp'hel Gonpa. The road followed the course of the sparkling Mekong River—Dza Chu in Tibetan—passing through the beautiful fields of that region. Along this road were many great monasteries, among them Sechhen Gonpa and, off the road, Dzogchhen Gonpa. I rejoiced to see that most were being reconstructed, for as soon as Chinese policy had shifted slightly toward tolerance the Tibetans began to rebuild. Though there were no longer great, wealthy families to sponsor these projects, support was widespread and even roadworkers, who labored for six yuan a day, offered what they could.

On the way we stopped in a little village. A messenger was sent to the monastery, about an hour away by horse, to notify my sister of our imminent arrival and to arrange for horses. While we waited, drinking tea in someone's house, a man started telling me about T'hrinlay Wangmo, hinting that she was a little crazy, crying all the time, saying wild things. As I listened, I did not know what to believe or to expect.

At last our escorts from the monastery arrived with the horses. Jigmed and Jane did not have a happy first encounter with Tibetan saddles. The cinch of Jigmed's saddle gave way and he fell to the ground; Jane quickly chose to dismount and walk after discovering that her saddle was a triangular construction of wood that sat on the horse like a pitched roof, padded with a single carpet. We rode near the ruins of the monastery that marks Gesar's birthplace, across the plains where his herds grazed, across a bridge and past a village just beyond the bridge. Tenp'hel Gonpa was several miles from this village and our procession moved slowly, delayed by people who ran up and bowed their head for blessing.

Finally we rounded the last bend and I glimpsed the monastery compound. Everything was as I remembered it, for the Chinese had not destroyed the buildings. Even the three-year retreat building was standing, its unadorned mud walls looking as if they should have washed away long ago. People lined up to receive my blessing, then broke ranks and followed us as we approached my sister's house. We reached her door with the crowd surging around us, and not until I had dismounted did I see the tiny woman who was too moved to speak. We touched foreheads and embraced, and she began to cry. We were quickly ushered inside by the lamas and monks, and offered tea.

T'hrinlay Wangmo stood less than five feet tall, yet she clearly commanded authority immensely greater than her stature. The lamas and monks of the monastery revered her, not only as her mother's daughter, but for her own qualities. They had brought her back to Tenp'hel Gonpa at great risk because she had offended the Chinese authorities repeatedly; they had built her house, and now they served her well. For her part, T'hrinlay Wangmo added a spark of crazy wisdom to their proceedings. People came to her for advice and prayers, just as they had come to her mother Dawa Drolma before her. I am sure that she gave them occasion to gossip because of her eccentric behavior, and I am not surprised that the man who talked to me while I waited for the horses thought she was slightly mad. I am also sure she occasionally exasperated the lamas and monks. Still, everyone at Tenp'hel Gonpa seemed to recognize that they had a jewel of the dharma in their midst, an authentic wisdom *dakini*.

Over the next two weeks, in conversations with her and with the lamas, her story unfolded. T'hrinlay Wangmo wept when she described the persecutions by the Chinese, and she repeated the same terrible stories over and over until I did not want to listen again. When the lamas told these stories, they always spoke in terms of her extraordinary powers as a *siddha* rather than her human suffering, as if she had transcended the physical experience of the beatings and torment. In her own accounts she did not obscure the miraculous displays of her realization, but she refused to deny her more ordinary experiences of pain, anger and sorrow. Both her qualities as a *dakini* and her experiences as a human being were encompassed by her vast understanding of the nondual nature of reality.

When, in my late teenage years, I left Tenp'hel Gonpa and went to Tromt'har, T'hrinlay Wangmo and my stepfather Sodga also moved away, relocating to Bumsar, the site of his monastery. As a great practitioner himself, he saw her special qualities and told her that she need never marry or live an ordinary life, that he would support her so that she could practice and do retreat. Not only did she reject this offer, she decided to take as her husband a man who had killed two people. This was totally unacceptable to Sodga, who refused to speak to or even look at her husband and severed relations with her as well. Sodga sought divinations from many lamas and the answer was always the same: if T'hrinlay Wangmo remained with her husband, it would be an obstacle to her practice and her longevity.

My sister had a fairly happy life with her husband for twenty-seven years, but in Sodga's view the match went from bad to worse because this man, who had killed two people, killed two more. When a lama's horse was stolen, he was among those who went out to track the thieves. A gunfight eventually broke out, and he shot the culprits. This was not uncommon in Kham—I had been in a similar situation myself—but it increased Sodga's contempt for his daughter's husband as a base murderer. At one point he actually assaulted the man, who did not retaliate because, as he told T'hrinlay Wangmo, "He is your father and he is a lama, and his beating may purify some of my bad karma." In twenty-seven years there was only one good moment between Sodga and T'hrinlay Wangmo. He summoned her one day and said, "Today you have the opportunity to retrieve one of your mother's *termas* if you follow my instructions exactly. The Chinese will be looking through some boxes of things they have looted. If you stand inconspicuously at the end of one box, a small case will fall out and you can snatch it unnoticed. Do this and bring the case to me." She did just as he said and retrieved the case, which she gave to Sodga. He said simply, "Today you have done well."

One day she entered his house in a rage, smashed every cup and dish he owned and left without explanation. A friend visited him shortly after and, surveying the wreckage, asked what had happened. "T'hrinlay Wangmo has done me a great service today," Sodga replied. Later that day he received from the Chinese a summons to appear before a tribunal; the next day he received a second letter informing him that there was no need to appear. In demolishing his crockery T'hrinlay Wangmo had purified the last vestiges of his karma to have to undergo such an ordeal.

Sodga lived very frugally—he spent almost everything he had on butter for butterlamps—and he was not a prominent lama whose prestige and wealth the Chinese felt compelled to destroy. In 1979 he died naturally in his bed. With his last breaths he said to T'hrinlay Wangmo, "If you love your dying father at all, you will not stay with that man." She agreed then to leave her husband, and she did.

DURING THE TWENTY-SEVEN-YEAR ESTRANGEMENT, Sodga broke his silence another time to warn T'hrinlay Wangmo to curb her hot tongue when dealing with the Chinese. She could not, and on at least three occasions they tried to kill her.

Once they ordered her to move rock with a crew for a bridge-building project. She refused, saying, "You can beat me and beat me again, but I will not move a pebble for you." Just as had happened in her previous life as Ugdrön, the strange *dakini* who lived by a bridge, they bound her hands and feet and threw her in the river. And, just as before, she did not sink, but floated upstream. Reluctantly, the Chinese allowed her to be fished out, and after that did not force her to work.

Another time, as she was riding her horse along the road, she was seized and brutally beaten by the highest Chinese official in the region. He used as his weapon the thick branch of a thorntree. She was not angry as he beat her, for she recognized the beating as karmic purification. In that tumultuous moment, she made a prayer that, by her suffering, others might be spared. When he thought he had beaten her to the brink of death, the official let her fall to the ground. To his amazement, she remounted her horse and, with the wild, triumphant yell that Khampas emit, she galloped away. The official jumped on his own horse and overtook her. He was amazed to see that the wounds had already healed. He invited her to stay at his house, and the next morning gave her six hundred yuan before sending her on her way, asking that she pray for him when he died. As it happened, the Chinese later summoned her to the regional capital and upon arrival, as she was walking to their offices, she passed a funeral procession.

"Who is that?" she asked.

"That is the governor of this region, who just died," she was told. T'hrinlay Wangmo began to pray, happy to be able to fulfill his request.

Yet another experience that T'hrinlay Wangmo described was witnessed by at least a hundred people. The Chinese had ordered everyone to pay homage to a photograph of Mao Zedong. T'hrinlay Wangmo refused, and instead reviled Mao as one who had caused the deaths of her relatives and friends. This public rebellion could not go unpunished, so the Chinese seized her, stripped her naked, drew a target on her chest and stood her before an executioner. As the crowd watched silently, the executioner fired. His gun merely clicked—no bullet shot forth. He fired a second time and again there was only a click. Then he test-fired his weapon in the air and the gun fired normally. Once more, he leveled the gun at T'hrinlay Wangmo and once more it did not fire. Thoroughly disgusted, he threw the gun on the ground and turned away.

The military officials seized T'hrinlay Wangmo, handcuffed her and marched her toward the prison. Suddenly, in front of the whole crowd, the iron handcuffs shattered into small pieces and fell to the ground. Her captors shoved her into the prison, where they held her overnight, then released her, ordering her to get out of their sight.

When asked what she was thinking as she stood before her executioner, she said, "I was thinking that I didn't care if they killed me because they had already killed so many of my relatives and friends."

A CONSTANT FLOW of visitors passed through my room in T'hrinlay Wangmo's house, offering a *katag* and one or two yuan, receiving a blessing cord, telling their stories. Everyone agreed that times had been terrible during the military consolidation of Chinese power and perhaps worse during the Cultural Revolution, but that now things were better. The monastery had survived because it was out of the way and no one had tried to defend it. The monks had simply vanished, returning to their own families. One of the *tulkus* had been captured, and the night before he was to be executed by drowning, he told those with him that he would not allow the Chinese to kill him. "What choice do you have?" they asked. "I have a choice," he replied. The next day, as he was being taken in a boat to deep, swift water, he transferred his consciousness through the practice of *p'howa*. In doing so, he prevented the Chinese from creating the terrible karma of murdering him.

Despite the Chinese injunction not to teach, I could not refuse. I learned that a group had entered three-year retreat with no teachings at all, just their faith. Secretly, I began to give them teachings on the preliminary practices. At Tenp'hel Gonpa the training of lamas and monks had been brought to a complete halt by the Chinese, and the texts destroyed. In a way, this was worse than the destruction of buildings.

One morning, toward the end of our stay at Tenp'hel Gonpa when I felt more secure that Chinese authority was at a safe distance, I was teaching the preliminaries in T'hrinlay Wangmo's house. A young lama came in fully dressed as a tantric practitioner, complete with a bone in his hair. As I taught he burst into tears and began to sob. He struggled to control himself and said, "I come from a place a long distance from here, and in that place there are no other lamas.

219

Everyone must rely on me and I have had no training, no teachings, not even these basic teachings on the preliminaries. Yet, when people die, their relatives come to me, trusting me to conduct the death ceremonies. It is not good, not for the dead person and not for me."

With that he broke down and began to sob again. I could not say much, because this is the great tragedy of Tibet, that even for those with faith, it is difficult to find the teachings. The great lineages will have to be reestablished from a few qualified teachers. It is my hope that they will be able to pass on the jewels of their knowledge and realization to practitioners who are courageous and able to persevere in the face of great obstacles, particularly the incursions of a modern, materialistic society into their culture.

IT WAS TIME to leave Tenp'hel Gonpa and travel on to Tromt'har and Nyagrong. T'hrinlay Wangmo did not want us to leave, of course, and we could overhear her telling her schemes to her monk-attendant late at night and him warning her that she could not hold us indefinitely. She made me sign a paper promising to come back in two years, a promise I was not able to keep although I did send my nephew, Lama Sonam Tsering, and yards of the best brocade, woven with Tibetan designs in Varanasi, India. One of the *tulkus* of Tenp'hel Gonpa, Tonpa Tulku, wanted to reestablish the tradition of Drukpa Kagyu lama dancing in the monastery and requested the brocades for making costumes.

When I said firmly that I was leaving and began talking to people about transportation, T'hrinlay Wangmo said, "You might as well wait here. There will be no truck for three days." I did not believe her, because a truck was scheduled to arrive the next day. She did not argue, but ordered tents and food for three days to be packed. We left on horses, except Jane, who was still leery of the Tibetan saddles and chose to walk, and the monks escorted us to the edge of the village. There, in unison, they prostrated to me, many with tears in their eyes. I inwardly made a commitment to help them as the opportunity arose.

We stopped briefly in the next village, then crossed the bridge to Gesar's plain. T'hrinlay Wangmo had arranged for three white tents to be pitched. We piled our luggage in the center of the largest tent and tied it all together with a primitive alarm system of dishes that would fall and clatter if sneak thieves came in the night.

T'hrinlay Wangmo proved right, and we slept in these tents for three nights until a truck arrived. The early September weather was rainy and cold, and at night there was the incessant barking of the pack of thirty or so dogs that roamed the plain. Yet here I came closest to experiencing the Tibet I remembered. The herdsmen had brought sheep down for the winter, and our tents were surrounded by thirty or forty others. There was visiting back and forth, a sense of leisure and open space, and food tasted very good. Most of all there was the powerful presence of the epic warrior Gesar, who as a child here had been surrounded by similar herds and tents.

The morning of our leaving was difficult, even though T'hrinlay Wangmo carefully contained her emotions. I wanted her to travel with us, but she refused because she said she would suffer violent motion sickness on the rough roads. She had completely endeared herself to Jigmed and Jane, since besides her fierce wrath, which we only heard about and did not experience, she had irresistible charm and had shown us very generous hospitality. They did not find it easy to leave and there was much needless fumbling with the luggage and attention to other mundane matters.

After some delay, as the trucks were pulling out, I looked at T'hrinlay Wangmo's face, expressionless except for her eyes. It was a moment of recognition of the forces of impermanence converging and of the unbreakable bond between us, a bond beyond time, space and circumstances. We nodded in polite farewell and each said our own silent prayers.

WE TRAVELED to Tromt'har next, riding in the cab of an empty logging truck. The evidence of rampant logging was everywhere, the rivers choked with logs flowing to China, the mountains stripped of the dense forests that had covered them when I left. The land looked to me like chemotherapy patients I had seen in the West—bald with a few wisps of hair. When I had asked my sister about it she had said, "People used to think that the local deities would be upset if the trees were cut, but the Chinese came, told them that nothing bad would happen and went ahead and cut. Now people are not so worried about the local deities because nothing did happen." Another person told me that the Chinese were trying to replant, but the seedlings did not survive.

At Tromt'har, the first person to greet me was my cousin, the one whom I had stabbed during a childish squabble more than five decades ago. Tears streaming down her face, she was overjoyed to see me. We walked up a hill, past the reconstructed Tromge Gonpa, to the house of my boyhood friend, Tulku Jigmed Namgyal. The house was simple, solid and commanded a sweeping view, over the rooftop of the monastery, of the mountains. As in Tenp'hel Gonpa, the stories unfolded in the course of conversations that continued for days.

Tromt'har suffered terribly during the initial Chinese subjugation and again during the Cultural Revolution. The Chinese looted the wealth and sacred objects of the region, and razed the monastery and its surrounding buildings. In the famine that followed in the early 1960s, many Tromge relatives died of starvation, including both my beautiful, kind auntie and my malicious, jealous auntie who had tried to rival my mother. Those who did not die were impoverished.

Tulku Jigmed Namgyal did not flee when the Chinese came. He worked as a woodcutter, a roadworker, a servant—whatever an ordinary man would do, he did better by working harder. He was a short, stocky man, and quite strong and capable. By his diligence he survived and supported his wife and four children. Yet, with the Cultural Revolution in 1966, a second wave of terror swept over the region and even his willingness to adapt to the Chinese rule could not protect him from their insane policies.

Late one night the family's dogs began to bark frantically. Peering out into the darkness, they saw that their tent was surrounded by a Chinese mob. Tulku Jigmed Namgyal put on his robes and quickly searched for some kind of weapon. Finding none, he went out into the night empty-handed. Just as a Chinese grabbed him, a neighbor thrust an iron bar in his hand and he fended off his assailant with a blow on the head. Others rushed him, and with superhuman strength, he threw them back. Someone handed him a hatchet and for a moment the attackers hesitated. The *tulku* broke away and ran.

The people threw themselves at the feet of the Chinese, crying and pleading that they not take him, that he was a good man, a poor man. Frustrated, one of the Chinese slammed his rifle butt into the abdomen of the *tulku*'s wife. She did not recover from this injury, but died leaving her two children behind, comforted only by the fact that when Tulku Arig heard the story, he said that Tulku Jigmed Namgyal would escape to safety.

The *tulku* fled to the forests of Golok and worked there as a laborer for twelve years, until the Chinese loosened their grip in the 1980s. His children fended for themselves, the oldest son T'hrinlay Odzer stepping into the role of father. The two of them were in Tromt'har at the time of my visit—T'hrinlay Odzer, a young lama and one of the dharma heirs of Tromge Gonpa, and his sister Kunlu, a nun who prepared food and served us with unstinting hospitality. Both seemed to have profound strength of character and hearts of refined gold.

When the *tulku* came back, he began to rebuild as quickly as resources allowed, using the offerings he received for ceremonies and prayers to buy materials. Tromge Gonpa, though incomplete, is twice as big as it was and better crafted. He also had new woodblocks carved for texts, put two *tulkus* into three-year retreat—finding support and retreat houses for them—and trained the monks and lamas of the monastery.

Four young lamas, all Tromge family relatives, are the Tromge Gonpa dharma heirs. Tulku Arig designated one of them, Tsultrim Lodrö, as the future abbot of the monastery, but the four treated one another strictly as equals. My son Jigmed Norbu found his peer group among these four lamas, with whom he felt a strong kinship. We considered arranging for Jigmed to return and join a retreat they would be undertaking. This did not happen—Jigmed's life took a different turn and he entered a three-year retreat in the United States—but a strong and enduring connection was established.

I was quite pleased with Jigmed throughout this trip. He was a natural traveler, observant, appreciative, quick to size up situations and capable in making arrangements. He had a quick temper at times, but a good heart. One day on a Chengdu city bus, a pickpocket tried to steal his money. Jigmed carried most of his money in a money belt, so all the thief got was a handful of coins and a punch in the ribs when Jigmed realized what was happening. When the other passengers tried to seize the man, however, Jigmed prevented it. Later he explained, "Who knows for how long the police might have thrown him in jail?"

ONE DAY we made a pilgrimage to Tulku Arig. Setting out on a hot, cloudless morning, we rode past the hill where Tromge Trungpa had been cremated, through the high meadows. Tulku Arig's retreat site was about three miles from Tulku Jigmed Namgyal's house, high on a hill. At the base of that hill, along a creek bed, about thirty tents had been pitched by gold miners. The night before, the Chinese had come, fired shots to chase away miners without licenses and seized one woman. The year before, a claim jumper had been killed, but greed for gold was insatiable. I reflected on the play of karmic forces that had brought the mining community and the retreat community to the same hill.

When we came in sight of the retreat house—really a hut surrounded by six or seven other huts and many prayer flags—I told everyone to dismount and walk as a respectful gesture to Tulku Arig and as a method of purification. Jane was having trouble with the altitude at Tromt'har, which is more than fourteen thousand feet, so the two of us kept the same pace while Jigmed went ahead with the other Tromge lamas. I could not walk more than fifty feet without sitting down for a rest.

It was a sign of Tulku Arig's meditative power that he had been able to practice in Tromt'har throughout the bad times, though on several occasions the Chinese sent Tibetan malcontents to harass him. The first, a woman, marched in, sat down and launched into a diatribe. Tulku Arig made no reply, but remained in immovable meditation. Finally, she fell silent, powerless to say more. The next day she returned and respectfully made an offering.

"Oh, no!" Tulku Arig protested. "If you come like this, the Chinese will be offended, and it will be hard on you. You must come as you did yesterday."

"I have no power to come as I did yesterday," she replied, and afterward she became a devoted follower of the dharma. A number of other people came with ill intentions, but if they were in Tulku Arig's presence only twice, they underwent a profound change of mind. Similarly, though Tibetans and Chinese alike destroyed wildlife in other regions—in the Tenp'hel Gonpa area thousands of prairie dogs and marmots had vanished—Tromt'har, under the influence of Tulku Arig, had become an unofficial wildlife refuge where people refrained from killing.

When we came to the last steep stretch up the hill, Tulku Arig's nephew came out, offered me a *katag* and escorted us into his small, cluttered room. He told me that I, but no one else, could see Tulku Arig. I asked him to make a request for Jigmed, Jane and Puge, a monk who had traveled with us from Tenp'hel Gonpa, but the answer was the same. So I went in while the others did prostrations and recited prayers outside.

As soon as I entered the room, he scolded me. "Why did you come with so many people?" Then he said, "Who are you?"

"Thubi," I answered, using my childhood nickname.

"Why did you go that way?" he demanded wrathfully.

For a moment I thought he meant why did I go the way of a *ngagpa* rather than maintaining my monk's vows, for he had given me those vows and I had not been able to return them to him directly, as is customary, on my way out of Tibet. Instead I had prayed strongly to Guru Rinpoche and returned them at Padma Kod, and afterward to my teacher Khanpo Dorje. Then I took his question to mean, why had I abandoned the life of a retreatant in Tibet? So I answered, "I left to escape the Chinese."

"Why escape? It wouldn't have been so bad if they caught you." With that, he said extensive long-life prayers for me. Finally he said, "Please don't insist that I see the others. You know that before I was in strict retreat and didn't see anybody. Now it is almost time for me to go, this year, next year. I must practice as much as I can. We won't see each other again. Now, don't stay longer. My practice time is being lost."

Already startled by his wrathful greeting and rather unhappy that he refused to see Jigmed and Jane, who had come so far to see him, I was shocked when he abruptly cut short our interview. Thoughts flooded my mind. "He is almost eighty years old and has been in retreat his whole life. Does he still hope to gain some greater realization in the little time he has left? Has he not yet passed beyond hope and fear?" Then I checked my mind. Tulku Arig had always ended his interviews like this, as a way of demonstrating the preciousness of each moment in the human body. Why, at the last minute, should he suddenly alter his habit? And suddenly I saw my own hope and fear, clinging to his physical presence as the lama, when truly, as a master of the Great Perfection teachings, he, his mind and his dharma teachings knew no boundaries of time and space. When I realized this, my mind relaxed into its natural awareness.

As I left, I requested that Tulku Arig bless Jigmed and Jane. As they listened outside his fence, he chanted long-life prayers and the blessing of Avalokiteshvara, his high, thin, but very vigorous voice piercing the midday sky.

For some days afterward I was disturbed by my encounter with Tulku Arig. If he disapproved of my not staying in retreat as a monk and leaving Tromt'har, then how much more would he disapprove of my emigrating to the West, marrying a Western woman and integrating my dharma activities into a Western context? Even I, then at the advanced age of fifty-seven and with the confidence of a great variety of life experiences, could not take lightly the disapproval of one of my spiritual fathers. To make things worse, I found myself constantly exasperated with Jane for no apparent reason other than the usual irritations of travel.

One morning she confronted me. "Are you sorry you gave back your monk's vows and married and went to the West?"

Looking into her anxious eyes, I felt the certainty of my answer and a deep inner calm. "Tulku Arig is a great and saintly lama, but I am immovable in what I have chosen to do." Again, as they had after seeing him, my hopes and fears fell away and I experienced the spacious expanse of pure awareness.

TULKU JIGMED NAMGYAL walked to the bus with us, leaning heavily on a cane he always used. He wept openly as he said good-bye. "You have been away so long and now you are leaving again. You must come back and teach." Deeply moved by his sincerity and kindness, I hoped to see him again and fulfill his request. However, in the following spring, T'hrinlay Odzer wrote me that his father had died unexpectedly, a few months after Tulku Arig's death, and he asked that I come to Tromt'har to continue the training that had been interrupted. Suddenly Tromt'har, so rich in the presence of those two great lamas, was bereft. My prayers were for the four young lamas, that they hold and increase their superb spiritual legacy.

OUR TRIP from Tromt'har to Chagdud Gonpa followed roughly the route I had taken after my first and second three-year retreats, though this time my means of transportation was not a horse but a logging truck ornamented with tin ridges and resembling a dinosaur, and an open trailer pulled by a small tractor that enveloped it with gas fumes. A few hours from Tromge monastery the road ran along the turbulent Nyagchu River, through logging camps and past the four-story houses of Nyagrong. The bottom floor of these houses shelters the animals, the second is used for grain and fodder storage, the third houses the family and the top floor has a shrineroom, a terrace and a loft to dry grain.

We were not sure how we would contact Chagdud Gonpa, but as soon as we reached Renub, the capital of Nyagrong and the town nearest the monastery, we met Anjang, one of the Gonpa's three main lamas and an extremely practical, capable administrator. He had been expecting us any day and immediately took over the arrangements, dispatching a monk back to the monastery while we went to a Chinese restaurant to have lunch. Then he traveled with us in the tractor-trailer to a place ten or fifteen miles down the road, to the trailhead of the path to the monastery.

Chagdud Gonpa stood several thousand feet above the river, accessible by a trail so steep that it was invisible from the road. Jigmed and Jane began hiking up while I waited for someone to bring a horse. As dark clouds swept across the late afternoon sky, I became concerned that we all reach shelter before we were overtaken by night or by one of Nyagrong's wild, sudden storms. At last several men arrived with a horse, and after helping me mount it, they led it up the path at a quick pace. When I reached our destination, I was relieved to find that Jigmed and Jane had arrived just before me and were comfortably drinking tea.

We stayed in the house in which I had been born in my previous lifetime as Chagdud Tanpai Gyaltsan. Surrounded by barley fields, with splendid views of the mountains, it was now inhabited by Gyurmed Dorje, an infallibly cheerful, good-hearted man and one of Chagdud Gonpa's three main lamas. Gyurmed was known as an accomplished scholar, Anjang for his skillful activity and a third lama named Ado for his qualities as a meditator. For generations Chagdud Gonpa had been held jointly by the families of these three lamas, who rotated the administration every three years. Usually the Chagdud *tulku* took rebirth in one of these families and received the highest honor as the head lama of the monastery though the administration continued to rotate. In my previous incarnation as Chagdud Tulku Tanpai Gyaltsan, I had been in Gyurmed Dorje's family, the brother of his father. Thus Gyurmed was my nephew, and because blood relationships endure across lifetimes, we still considered each other uncle and nephew even though in this life I had taken rebirth in the Tromge family. The combination of family lineage and *tulku* lineage made Chagdud Gonpa extremely strong and stable. During my long absence, Gyurmed Dorje, Anjang and Ado fully cooperated and, with the help of the monks and villagers, had managed to protect Chagdud Gonpa and all its possessions during the years of Chinese oppression. The texts, ritual implements, silks and statues had been distributed to monks and villagers, who, at great personal risk, hid them until the bad times passed. Most importantly, no one allowed himself to be coerced into denouncing the monastery or its lamas. Anjang, however, spent seven years in prison for his dharma activities. Chagdud Gonpa had not been destroyed from the inside out as other monasteries had.

A Tibetan from another region, however, did attempt to destroy the large, clay statues that remained behind in the monastery, particularly an old, very sacred Guru Rinpoche statue in the dharma protector shrineroom. He came and found the heavy wooden doors locked, so he climbed up to the small windows under the roof and was about to enter when he saw a large tiger—a vision, but completely real to him—leap in front of the statue. He fled, and afterward became very ill, vomiting blood.

Still not convinced of the power of the dharma protectors, he returned and using authority invested in him by the Chinese, ordered the doors opened. Inside he saw a shiny black rock slightly larger than a man's head. "What is this?" he demanded.

"It is the life force stone of the dharma protectors," someone replied.

"Don't tell stupid lies," the would-be saboteur said harshly. "What dharma protectors? What life force? This is a rock— only a rock—that I will take outside now and throw away."

He reached down and seized it, but it did not move. He ordered another man to help him, then another and another. When four men could not lift the stone, he stepped back and started to mutter incoherently. At that moment, at a distant spot on the riverbank, his son fell into the water and drowned. The man lost his sanity and never regained it. The Chinese and their henchmen scoffed at the idea that these events were related, but no one had much personal enthusiasm for destroying Chagdud Gonpa after that.

WE STAYED at Gyurmed Dorje's house for about a week while the monks arranged things at the monastery up the mountain. Originally they had wanted to make elaborate ceremonies in both Kanze and Renub, but I refused, not wanting to rile the Chinese. Now they were planning a procession from Gyurmed Dorje's house to Chagdud Gonpa and ceremonies in the monastery.

On the morning of the event we awakened early and dressed. This was not a simple matter. Jane, who had brought only Western travel clothes, borrowed Tibetan-style clothing from Jigmed, and Jigmed, at the insistence of Anjang and Gyurmed Dorje, dressed in borrowed clothes as a monk. I, too, was given a set of clothes to wear—a full *chuba* instead of my usual informal half-*chuba* (wraparound skirt).

We mounted horses outside Gyurmed Dorje's house and set off to Chagdud Gonpa, a mile or so away and situated on the highest ridge of the mountain. A large contingent of lay people silently followed the ranks of the monks and lamas who led our horses and carried our baggage. Outside the village we encountered the first of a series of pyres burning fragrant incense cedar. At moments the gray, early-morning fog that trailed up the mountainside and the smoke from the cedar pyres clasped like spectral fingers, enveloping everything. In the distance the long horns signaled our approach, their great tides of sound swelling and ebbing, accompanied by cymbals and deep drums, conch shells and oboes whose high, thin melody sliced through the mountain air.

In my past incarnations I had been in such processions many times, tributes not just to me but to the powerful dharma commitments maintained by the lamas and monks at Chagdud Gonpa that compelled me to return lifetime after lifetime, and in this lifetime to return from a distant land and an alien culture. The monastery had been destroyed twice since its founding by Chagdud Sherab Gyaltsan; my own time there had not always been easy. Yet the pure spiritual intention of that first Chagdud in establishing Chagdud Gonpa had endured for centuries, made manifest through bloodline and lineage, and the monastery itself had miraculously survived the indiscriminate desecration of Tibet by the Chinese. As we approached, faith and joy flooded my mind.

We rode past a line of a hundred monks to the monastery's courtyard and dismounted from our horses. A monk ran up to hold a large golden umbrella over Jigmed. At first I thought a mistake had been made, since the umbrella is held over the head lama. However, as we entered the temple door one lama asked if today Jigmed might sit on the high throne. I said nothing, and as Jigmed was ushered to the throne and I to the lower one next to it, I realized that the three lamas had decided among themselves to use this ceremony to recognize my son as the next throneholder of Chagdud Gonpa. Jigmed was quite shocked, but my own reactions were mixed—I felt unhappy because the lamas had not discussed their plans with me before, concerned about Chinese retaliation because they had specifically prohibited enthronement ceremonies and pleased that Jigmed should receive this honor. At a deeper level I wondered if this ceremony would really create the interdependence they hoped for, if Jigmed would really hold Chagdud Gonpa in Tibet or if his karmic destiny lay elsewhere.

The lamas offered to Jigmed a mandala—a symbolic representation of all the wealth of the universe—and a bell and *dorje* (a scepter symbolic of mind's absolute nature). Then they made speeches. Anjang spoke first to me: "You have been away so long that seeing you is like the living meeting the dead." He continued in the same vein, concluding with a formal request that Jigmed, as my son and representative, come to Chagdud Gonpa as throneholder.

Two or three days after the ceremony, at the lamas' insistence, I gave a long-life empowerment. The Chinese repeatedly forbade empowerments of any kind but I could not refuse. I only asked that it be done secretly, and for the monks alone. They agreed to this stipulation.

On the day of the empowerment, however, I saw throngs of people gathering in the courtyard in front of the monastery. Many of the monks had told their immediate family and those family members had told other relatives, and now I faced the prospect of giving an empowerment to four hundred people. As we entered the monastery, Jane, who was extremely anxious, said that I should not give it, but I resolved to ignore the danger and assume that this was meant to happen. I took my place on the throne and began to perform the preliminary phase of the empowerment while the Chagdud Gonpa monks solemnly seated themselves. This quiet, orderly moment gave way to an uproar an instant later, when the huge wooden doors of the shrineroom suddenly heaved open and the crowd rushed in. The monks bolted from their places and pushed people back; the *gekös* (disciplinarians) waved big sticks and whacked them against the posts of the shrineroom. Afraid they might really hit people, I called out for them to stop, then realized it was all an act, staged so I would not think they had simply invited this crowd—their families—to participate. They all settled down, and without comment I proceeded to give the empowerment.

For the next few days I looked around Chagdud Gonpa, and was very pleased that things had generally remained intact. Of course, they were not perfect. The roof was in dire need of repair—it would be a great irony if the elements destroyed what the Chinese had spared. More importantly, although some training of monks and lamas had continued in secrecy during the years of oppression, now it needed to expand to meet the needs of the new generation before the older, more knowledgeable lamas such as Gyurmed Dorje passed away. I committed myself to the establishment of a *shedra,* a school where the Buddha's doctrine could be taught fully. Before we left Chagdud Gonpa, all the monks and lamas assembled for a long meeting. One after another they stood up and said basically the same thing: I had been gone too many years, and now that I was back I must stay and teach, or if I could not stay this time, I must come again soon and stay longer to teach. At one point the Gonpa's oldest monk stood up—the monk who had traveled to Tromt'har with Chagdud Tanpai Gyaltsan—and began by saying, "I never doubted that this Chagdud Tulku is who he is, because I was with him in his last life when he gave Delog Dawa Drolma, the one who became his mother, that gold and silver *gau.*" Then he, too, asked me to stay or to return and teach, though surely he would soon make his own journey across the threshold of death.

Jane made a brief speech, which I translated, saying that Chagdud Gonpa in Tibet had been the inspiration for establishing Chagdud Gonpa in the West, and that inspiration had deepened for her when she saw the monastery and learned of the loyalty of the monks and lay people during the years of Chinese domination. She concluded by saying that now that they had met, she hoped the bond between the two *gonpas,* East and West, would grow stronger to the benefit of both.

Jigmed spoke, promising to help Chagdud Gonpa and to stay there as time and circumstances allowed. Then I spoke, reiterating my intention to benefit as I could.

At last we departed with a group of the younger monks to make a pilgrimage around Shangnang Dragkar, a nearby mountain sacred to Guru Rinpoche. We went down the steep backside of the Chagdud Gonpa mountain, the monks holding me aloft on a platform. At a village at the foot of the mountain, a large crowd had gathered, including Gyurmed Dorje's father, my brother in my previous incarnation, who greeted me as casually as if I had come back from a day trip to Renub. I performed another long-life empowerment—by now caution had been thrown to the winds—and these people then made an extremely generous offering to my own long life.

In Nyagrong there are no large herds of animals, and a family that has a yak or a few sheep is considered very fortunate. To increase my long life, many people offered to refrain from killing their animals and to dedicate the merit of this virtue to my longevity. I was deeply moved by this gesture, for it meant that they would be giving up scarce meat and the valuable use of skins.

For the next two days we made a pilgrimage around the sacred mountain, passing razed and pillaged monasteries, staying overnight in a small monastery deep in the forest where seven old monks and nuns were in continual retreat, and at last circumambulating the peak. The pilgrimage was arduous for Jigmed, Jane and me, and grueling for the uncomplaining monks who had to pack our supplies and baggage and cook. Still, they were young and high-spirited, and at the end we had established the affectionate bonds that develop among companions on a spiritual journey. We concluded the pilgrimage with prayers and a group picture, then traveled down to the road where the three of us took a jeep back to Renub.

In Renub we were summoned for joint meetings with the Tibetan Reception Committee and Chinese officials, and felt considerable anxiety because of Jigmed's enthronement and the empowerments I had given. Their agenda, however, was our affirmation of the people's freedom, and they reiterated over and over that the bad times had passed and now the people were content. Their very insistence became oppressive, as though they hoped to indoctrinate us.

It was pointless to dispute them, however, and we didn't. We simply told them how happy we were to see the rebuilding of monasteries and to see people practice their religion openly. These officials, however, had no knowledge of true freedom, mind's ultimate freedom, freedom that cannot be diminished for the spiritual practitioner who has attained it no matter how oppressive the outer circumstances. Their idea of freedom was a slightly less restrictive policy here, a new permission there. We could rejoice to the extent that these policies caused less harm and allowed more virtue to flourish, but we did not mistake them for freedom itself.

From Renub we returned to Kanze and from there we made the four-day journey to Chengdu and checked into the huge, comfortable Jin Jiang Hotel. The hotel was swarming with reporters from all over the world, covering an uprising in Lhasa that had sent shock waves throughout China. We were asked what we knew, and of course we knew nothing of Lhasa, so far from Kham. Even what we knew of Kham seemed tentative, fading like a dream in morning. For a few days we rested, then traveled on to meet a group of my American students who had come to China to make a pilgrimage to the sacred five peaks of Wu Tai Shan, where centuries before one of the Buddha's most profound practice lineages had passed from master to master, then was carried to India, Tibet and, eventually, to America.

Glossary

absolute reality   the pure, unchanging, indestructible, indivisible essence of being, which is beyond concept or confusion

arak (Tib., *a-rag*)   whiskey

Avalokiteshvara (Skt.; Tib., *Kyanrazig, spyan-ras-gzigs*) bodhisattva of compassion, embodying the compassion of all buddhas and bodhisattvas

baksheesh (Hindi)   a bribe

bardo (Tib.)   intermediate state; various transitions the consciousness makes in the cycle of existence, including the *bardo* of one's lifetime, the dream *bardo,* the *bardo* of the moment of death, the *bardo* of the true nature of reality, the *bardo* of becoming and the *bardo* of meditation

bep (Tib., *'bebs*)   in Tibetan yoga, a controlled fall that channels the body's subtle energies through the subtle channels to promote higher states of awareness

bodhisattva (Skt.)   in Mahayana Buddhism, one whose conduct and realization are in accord with the altruistic intention to work for the welfare of sentient beings until all without exception reach enlightenment

Bon, Bonpo (Tib.)   an ancient shamanistic tradition that predates Buddhism in Tibet; a Bonpo is a practitioner of Bon

Buddhism, Hinayana (Skt., lit. "the lesser vehicle")   the practice path of personal salvation in which the practitioner seeks to escape the suffering of the cycles of existence through renunciation and completely cutting any attachment to worldly appearances

Buddhism, Mahayana (Skt., lit. "the greater vehicle")   the practice path of those who seek liberation from suffering not only for themselves, but for all sentient beings; the Mahayana ideal is the heroic practitioner who turns back from the total peace of nirvana until all beings reach enlightenment

Buddhism, Vajrayana   (Skt., lit. "the vehicle of the indestructible nature of being")   a branch of Mahayana practiced by those who seek to know the absolute nature of being through the very direct methods passed through the lineages of Vajrayana teachers; often referred to as the "short path"

butterlamp   a votive lamp made of metal that burns melted butter or oil

chang (Tib.)   beer made from fermented grain, often barley

chod (Tib., *gcod*; lit. "to cut")   the practice of ultimate generosity in which the practitioner offers everything, even his or her own body, to whomever might partake of it, but particularly to the demons of conditioned existence

chodpa, chodma   (Tib., *gcod-pa, gcod-ma*)   a male or female practitioner of chod, respectively

chuba (Tib., *chu-pa*)   the various outer robes worn by both men and women in Tibet

dakini (Skt.; Tib., *khadro, mkha'-'gro;* lit. "sky goer," "sky dancer")   the feminine aspect of pristine awareness

delog (Tib., *'das-log*)   one who physically dies for an extended period of time but whose consciousness, after experiencing other realms of being, returns and reanimates the body

dharma king   a king who uses his worldly power to create spiritual benefit according to the teachings of the sacred dharma

dharma protector (Skt., *dharmapala*)   a deity pledged to guard practitioners on the path against obstacles

dri (Tib., *'bri*)   the female of the species known as "yak," the Tibetan word "yak" referring only to the male; a large oxlike animal with long hair

dualism   in Tibetan Buddhism, the fallacy of perceiving reality divided into subject (self) and object (other)

dur (Tib.)   a ceremony to expel negative entities, usually on the day a corpse is taken to the graveyard

dutzi (Tib., *bdud-rtsi*)   sacred substances that have been consecrated to imbue them with the power to liberate whoever tastes them from suffering

emanation (Tib., *tulpa, sprul-pa*)   a being who is a direct manifestation of the enlightened intention of a buddha or bodhisattva

empowerment (Tib., *wang, dbang*)   a ceremony during which a realized lama authorizes a practitioner to meditate

241

on a specific deity by transmitting the blessing of the lineage and by invoking the qualities of the deity's body, speech and mind

gau (Tib., *ga'u*)   reliquary; a locketlike container that holds consecrated substances and sacred relics

Gelug (Tib., *dge-lugs*)   one of the four major traditions of Tibetan Buddhism

gegan (Tib., *dge-rgan*)   one who teaches reading, writing, crafts and other secular subjects; in a monastery, a *gegan* might also teach various aspects of ritual and liturgy

gonla (Tib., *mgon-bla*)   in Tibetan monasteries, a practitioner whose official function is to perform extensive daily prayers and offerings to the dharma protectors

Guru Rinpoche   *see* Padmasambhava

Kagyu (Tib., *bka'-brgyud*)   one of the four major traditions of Tibetan Buddhism

kangling (Tib., *rkang-gling*)   the trumpet, made of a human thighbone, used by *chod* practitioners to summon beings to the offering of a feast; a metal horn used in Vajrayana rituals

karma (Skt.)   the inevitability of cause and effect whereby virtue engenders happiness and nonvirtue engenders suffering

katag (Tib., *kha-btags*)   a long, white or sometimes blue ceremonial scarf offered to a lama or exchanged by lamas as a symbol of purity

Khampa (Tib., *khams-pa*)   someone from Kham, the eastern region of Tibet that borders China

khanpo (Tib., *mkhan-po*)   the highest degree conferred on a religious scholar

lineage, lineage holder   the unbroken line of dharma transmission from teacher to student from the time of the historical Buddha Shakyamuni down to the present; a lineage holder is one who has received the lineage transmission from his or her own teacher, attains a high degree of realization of the practice and is thus capable of teaching it to others

Losar (Tib., *lo-gsar*)   Tibetan New Year

Madhyamaka (Skt.)   the "Middle Way" school of Mahayana Buddhist philosophy that deals with the nature of reality as transcending existence and nonexistence

mala (Skt.)   a rosary usually with 108 or 111 beads, used to count mantra repetitions

mandala (Skt.)   a sacred configuration that depicts the enlightened state of mind through various graphic elements such as colors and the forms of deities; alternatively, an arrangement of offerings that the practitioner envisions as including the entire universe and all its contents transformed into boundless sensory delights

mani (Tib.) **wall**   a wall built of stones inscribed with the mantra of the deity Avalokiteshvara, *Om Mani Padme Hung*

Manjushri (Skt.)   the bodhisattva of transcendent knowledge embodying the wisdom of all buddhas and bodhisattvas

mantra (Skt.)   specific phrase used to invoke enlightened beings or to accomplish the transformative activities of enlightened mind

mirror *puja*   a divination ceremony in which the interdependence of mind's natural qualities of awareness and clairvoyance and the power of a realized lama's ritual and prayers enable a seer to foretell events by looking on the surface of a mirror

meditation box a piece of furniture with a high back, a cushioned platform seat and a built-in tabletop that serves as both a throne and a bed for retreatants

mindstream (Tib., *semgyud, sems-rgyud;* lit. "thread of consciousness") the continuum of one's consciousness throughout the cycles of birth and death

naga (Skt.) species of supernatural serpentlike animals associated with environmental harmony

ngagpa, ngagma (Tib., *sngags-pa, sngags-ma*) a male or female Vajrayana practitioner, respectively, who practices the very swift, easy path of the mantra (*ngag*) vehicle; popularly refers to a practitioner who has a wife or husband or consort

nirvana (Skt.) a state beyond the cycles of conditioned existence associated with peace and everlasting bliss

nyam (Tib., *nyams*) an extraordinary but temporary state of mind, such as the arising of a vision, that is a result of meditation but does not constitute full, stable realization

Nyingma (Tib., *rnying-ma*) the oldest of the four major traditions of Tibetan Buddhism, based primarily on the lineage transmissions of Padmasambhava

Padmasambhava (Skt.) also known as Guru Rinpoche, the saint who brought Vajrayana Buddhist teachings from India and propagated them in Tibet in the eighth century

p'howa (Tib., *'pho-ba*) the transference of consciousness, particularly transference at the moment of death into a pureland or other states of higher awareness

p'hurba (Tib., *phur-pa*) a ritual dagger with a three-sided blade, which represents the liberation of the three mental poisons of anger, grasping and stupidity

prayer wheel a cylinder filled with mantras, spun by hand as a religious exercise

preliminary practices (Tib., *ngondro, sngon-'gro*) the meditations that consitute the introduction to Vajrayana practice: 100,000 full-length prostrations during the recitation of a refuge prayer; 100,000 recitations of a prayer that affirms the altruistic intention to practice until all beings attain enlightenment; 100,000 Vajrasattva purification mantras; 100,000 mandala offerings; 100,000 recitations of the guru yoga mantra

prostration a bow of homage to the Three Jewels and Three Roots, either by stretching one's body full length upon the ground (full prostration) or by kneeling and touching one's head, knees and hands to the ground (short prostration)

puja (Skt.) worship, usually performed as a group religious ceremony

pureland an environment of enlightened being in which the sacred dharma is perfectly expressed in every facet of that environment

rainbow body a term referring to the two categories of dissolution of a very great meditator's physical body at the moment of death, one in which the body dissolves, leaving only nails and hair behind, and one in which the practitioner attains the power to manifest as a light body

realization holder (Tib., *rigdzin, rig-'dzin;* lit. "one who holds intrinsic awareness") a practitioner who has so thoroughly integrated Vajrayana practice into his or her mind that he or she recognizes the very nature of mind and reality

relative reality the changeable, unstable, composite appearances that arise when one holds as true the seeming duality of subject and object

Rimé (Tib., *ris-med*) the ecumenical tradition of Tibetan Buddhism

root teacher the teacher who introduces the practitioner to the nature of mind

sadhu (Skt.) in India, a wandering, mendicant yogi

Sakya (Tib., *sa-skya*) one of the four major traditions of Tibetan Buddhism

samsara (Skt.) the cycle of conditioned existence associated with endless suffering due to delusion

sangyum (Tib., *gsang-yum*; lit. "secret mother") the consort of a highly realized male practitioner; in more general usage, the wife of a high lama

satsa (Tib., *satstsha*) clay or other pliable substances molded into the shape of a *stupa*

seed syllable a Sanskrit syllable that in meditation symbolizes the meditator's intrinsic awareness and in developing-stage practice serves as the basis for the visualization of a deity

siddha (Skt.) one who has attained supernormal powers through meditative realization

siddhi (Skt.) the powers attained through meditative realization, generally classified as ordinary *siddhis* (psychic powers and various supernormal manipulations of phenomena) and the sublime *siddhi* (enlightenment)

stupa (Skt.) a monumental structure whose architectural elements symbolize the thirty-seven factors conducive to enlightenment

sutras (Skt.) discourses of the Buddha Shakyamuni

tantras (Skt.) the esoteric texts that form the basis of Vajra-yana theory and practice

terma (Tib., *gter-ma*) treasure; teachings concealed until a time when they will be practiced with more benefit; primarily classified as earth treasures and mind treasures

terton (Tib. *gter-ston*) treasure revealer; one who by power of realization discovers and opens a terma

Three Jewels buddha, dharma and sangha; the central principles of Buddhism, buddha being a fully enlightened state of mind, dharma being the teachings that comprise the path to enlightenment and sangha being the community of dharma practitioners on the path

Three Roots lama, *yidam* and *dakini;* the central principles of Vajrayana Buddhism, the lama being the root of blessing, the *yidam* being the root of realization and the *dakini* being the root of enlightened activity

t'hangka (Tib., *thang-ka*) Tibetan Buddhist scroll painting

tsampa (Tib., *rtsam-pa*) barley, dry-roasted and ground into flour; kneaded into a dough with hot salted tea and butter, it is a staple food in Tibet

tsog (Tib., *tshogs*) a gathering, usually an offering ceremony in which substances are assembled, consecrated, offered to the buddhas and bodhisattvas who embody enlightenment and partaken of by the participants in the ceremony

tulku (Tib., *sprul-sku*)   a recognized incarnation of a high lama

tummo (Tib., *gtum-mo*)   in Tibetan yoga, the practice of generating inner heat

umzé (Tib., *dbu-mdzad*)   chant leader

vajra **master**   the lama who presides over a Vajrayana ritual

Vajrapani   the bodhisattva of spiritual power, who brought the tantras into the human realm

Vajrasattva   the deity who embodies the innate purity of absolute mind; the preliminary practice involving meditation on Vajrasattva is used to purify the defilements of one's ordinary mind

wrathful deity   an aspect of enlightenment embodying qualities appropriate for direct intervention in overcoming the mind's poisons of anger, grasping, stupidity, jealousy and pride

yaksha (Skt.)   one of a class of harm-causing spirits

yeti (Nepalese)   a mysterious, rarely sighted animal that lives in Tibet

yidam (Tib.)   meditational deity; the deity a practitioner meditates on to realize his or her own perfect qualities as that deity

zen (Tib., *gzan*)   a long piece of cloth Buddhist practitioners wrap around their upper body